HOW I DIED AT AGE 36 BUT WILL LIVE FOREVER

A tale about practical spirituality and estate planning

Anastasia Fainberg

LANDON
HAIL
PRESS

Paperback ISBN: 978-1-959955-94-8
Hardback ISBN: 978-1-959955-95-5

Published by Landon Hail Press
Book cover design by Rich Johnson, Spectacle Photo
Back cover photo by Angelli Nguyen

To my children, Daniel, Raphael, and Adele,
who first showed me what unconditional love feels like,
and through whom I learned that love is not something we
create, but something that moves through us
when we stop resisting it.
You were my first teachers,
and it was through loving you that the question arose:
How can this same love be lived for all?
And to God,
not as something outside of me,
but as the same living presence that looks through my eyes,
moves my hands, and poured itself out as these pages.
This book is not an offering to You,
but an expression of You.
Namaskār.

"When I am no longer here,
I will sing through the voices of my children,
and then their children...
We are just switching places.
That's the law of Samsara—the never-ending circulation of people."

—"Samsara," Russian song by Basta (trans. by author)

Contents

Foreword 1

From the Author 5

Chapter 1: Introduction: 3 Levels of Spiritual Knowledge 7

Chapter 2: My Story of Finding this Path 13

1994 13

2005 17

2008 21

2011 23

2015-2019 25

2022 27

Turn to Spirituality 30

Enlightenment: What It Means and How It Applies to this Teaching. 36

Chapter 3: Concept 1 of the Teaching:

Space/Consciousness 38

Where Does God Exist? 38

Where Does "I" Exist? 48

Is "I" a Personality? 51

Where is "I" in the Dream Space? 52

Non-duality of All Being 56

Why Does Duality Appear in Oneness? 64

How is Duality Shaped in Humans? 68

Chapter 4: Concept 2 of the Teaching: The
Doer/Chooser/Actor 74
Understanding How the "I" Continues to Exist 83
"I" in a child 83
"I" Opposite "Others" 85
"I" in relationships 87
"I" in time 87
Chapter 5: Practices to Integrate the Teaching 94
Attuning to the Body 94
Deepening the Awareness of the Body 96
From Mental Description to Direct Perception 97
Becoming Aware of Space and the Silent Field of
Perception 99
Neti Neti 102
Expanding Awareness Beyond Body 103
Dark and Silent Retreat 106
Chapter 6: Concept 3 of the Teaching: Effortless
Manifestation 109
True Manifesting is Altruism 110
Manifesting in Business 114
Manifesting in Relationships 118
Manifesting Desired Objects 124
Chapter 7: 3 Levels of Estate Planning 129
The Relative Still Matters 129
The First, Most Basic Level: No Plan at All 131
Middle Level: The Will-Based Plan 137

Mature, Highest Level: A Trust-Based Plan ______ 144
Why This Matters Even in Non-Dual Understanding ______ 149
Why I Do This Work ______ 151
Chapter 8: Why this Book is the Ultimate, Non-compromising, Radical Truth ______ 153
Conclusion ______ 161
Afterword ______ 164
About the Author ______ 166

Foreword

THERE IS NO SHORTAGE of information available in today's connected age. Curiously, there's also no one handbook to help give us advice on how to live a rich, joyful, and fulfilling life. Imagine being given a manual of instructions at the same time as a birth certificate!

And yet, the universe conspired and led you right here, right now, to this work and these words you are reading—or listening to—in this moment.

Let me be the first to congratulate you on investing energy in its ideas, concepts, and story.

For some, it will be a first step into the realm of self-discovery. For others, it may be a gentle reminder of its precepts and concepts. Above all, it is both familiar and unique, like all great art.

To read a book isn't unlike planning a Family Trust. Anastasia eloquently gets to this in ways I'd never considered, as you'll discover in its subsequent chapters. It begins with an intention—perhaps the result of months of "meaning to get to it" or "waiting for the right time to start." Then, it becomes a quest of discovery.

In the case of both the journey of self and of creativity, properly planning for your family needs a collaborator—a mentor with knowledge and insight around the nuances of the rule of law, coupled with an understanding and relatable touch.

My intention in my first meeting with Anastasia to help with our family's trust was simple: I had no idea what I was doing! Who could help me discover the path? By the time we had our first conversation, it was the result of our combined experiences—of both our physical and spiritual lives—leading to a point of intersection.

It felt, as I would find out from others who had worked with Anastasia, like it was meant to happen.

After many years plugged into the American capitalistic system, full of its ebbs and flows and my own wavering relationship with money, I'd found myself thinking about the future in a way I never had.

Suddenly, I'd stopped hustling and running long enough to find myself with a modicum of wealth. And with it came a question I'd never suspected I'd have: how would the legacy of my own materialistic earnings live on, once my physical body is no longer "here"?

Death in the North American culture has traditionally held a finite state. Yet there are many deaths before our physical one. The death of worry and of ego and of that anxiety became an amalgam of both my spiritual and materialistic selves.

Completing a trust helped put an end to something I didn't even realize was a part of my anxiety: that nagging, constant unknowing of what would be the final outcome for my years of hard work and, dare I say the word so richly used in the spiritual world, suffering.

Reading this work is a journey into the author's lived experience as well as the parallel story each of us holds.

There is value in remembering that the path is both unique and also exactly the same for all creatures on this Earth.

My advice is to take a deep breath and reread parts of this book in their entirety, if necessary. Above all else, let go of the patterns and loops that no longer serve your greater purpose of enlightenment and inner peace.

There's that phrase that has recently been so vital to my life—*let go*. It's a powerful statement with different implications, dependent upon its context. Within this book are many powerful concepts richly told through the lens of Anastasia's experience.

My hope is that its gifts help propel you on your own journey toward peace and fulfillment in both the physical and spiritual realms. The power is within and, also, without.

Greg Hoy
Entrepreneur, Musician, Seeker
Boulder, Colorado
April 2026

From the Author

HAVE YOU EVER pondered the concepts of life and death?

I should probably rephrase and say, "Who hasn't pondered the concepts of life and death?" Because, realistically, there is probably not a single person who has ever lived who has not thought about life and death and the overall meaning of both.

On the one hand, I am a what you would call a "seeker": one of those people who has been tirelessly and relentlessly searching for answers about the great scheme of things—life, death, and the meaning and purpose to both. I have read numerous books, attended numerous retreats, researched and participated in some aspects of all major world religions, paid thousands of dollars to spiritual gurus, and engaged in dozens of forms of meditation and other spiritual practices.

On the other hand, I am a trained lawyer, one who always looks for a logical explanation, who does not believe anything without reasonable proof based on facts, and who questions everything in a rational and scientific way. Distortions, illogical stories, fantasies, and things that don't add up rationally or that I cannot perceive and confirm with my own five senses just don't do it for me.

Now, at age thirty-seven, having searched for spiritual answers for at least twenty years and having practiced the law for eleven years, I have finally found the Truth. Some call it enlightenment; some refer to it as the knowledge or spiritual awakening. But whatever term is used is of no meaning. As this book will explain further, enlightenment is not something that puts one into a state of constant bliss, where you leave the worldly life and live in a state of Nirvana somewhere in the Himalayas. Instead, enlightenment truly is just understanding of one's true nature, while applying that understanding to one's worldly life. No fireworks, no altered state of consciousness, no other fancy attributes we would normally associate with spiritual awakening. It's just a state of being as you are. Pure and simple, but so fulfilling, so sweet, and so peaceful…

So, this book is about a rational mind finding and utilizing the highest spiritual truth. The truth that gives peace of mind and a complete sense of being content with everything there is, while also logically making sense and staying applicable in our regular day-to-day worldly lives.

This book also explores the three tiers of estate planning as they relate to the three tiers of spiritual awareness. It draws parallels between spiritual concepts and the key concepts of planning for life and death.

If you are a spiritual seeker but have a rational mind and cannot find your place of peace and contentment in the diverse scope of religious dogmas, this book is for you. If you are a rational planner who wants to leave a conscious legacy in this worldly life, this book is for you. Or if you are simply intrigued by the title and want to know what I mean by "dying but living forever," you may also find this book quite interesting.

This book will not disappoint.

~Anastasia Fainberg, author

Chapter 1

Introduction

3 Levels of Spiritual Knowledge

AS I STATED BEFORE, this book is not for everyone. Just as my estate planning practice is not for everyone. Even though you will realize, by reading the part of this book that outlines the Teaching, the ultimate truth of complete, undividable unity of all there is on the relative/human plane of existence, there are multiple layers and levels of variation in the physical manifestations of that unity. This part of the book will first briefly outline the three levels of spirituality as they apply to the three levels of human intelligence/minds.

All spiritual traditions are like ladders leading to the same place: your true, original nature. Different religions give this truth different names. In Hinduism, it's Brahman, Vishnu, and Shiva. In Christianity, it is the Father, Son, and Holy Spirit. In Buddhism, Dharmakaya, Sambhogakaya, and Nirmanakaya.

The words vary, but the essence is the same: there are three variables that must be in place for this reality to exist—emptiness, awareness, and the potential to create the world of forms. Always the holy triad. Together, they describe your true nature, as if reality can only speak about itself in a threefold way.

In Hinduism, this appears as Brahman, Vishnu, and Shiva. Brahman as the formless, infinite ground of being; Vishnu as the sustaining intelligence that preserves and permeates creation; and Shiva as the power through which forms dissolve and return to their source. In Christianity, the same structure emerges as the Father, Son, and Holy Spirit. The Father represents the unmanifest source beyond form; the Son embodies that source made visible in the world of form; and the Holy Spirit is the living, animating presence that moves through creation, breathing life into matter.

Buddhism articulates this triad with remarkable precision through the three kāyas: Dharmakāya, the empty, boundless nature of mind; Sambhogakāya, the luminous, knowing aspect of awareness; and Nirmāṇakāya, the manifest world of forms, bodies, and appearances. The distinctions exist only as a way of pointing, not as divisions in reality itself.

Whether we call it God, Brahman, Buddha, consciousness, or space, the message is consistent: for reality to appear at all, there must be an open ground, a knowing presence, and the creative potential through which forms arise. Names and symbols vary, rituals differ, and doctrines diverge, but the underlying architecture remains unchanged. Everywhere we look, various religious traditions are pointing to the same holy triad: emptiness as the ground, awareness as the knower, and creative potential as the movement through which the world comes into being.

So, why do traditions talk about these aspects as gods with specific forms and stories? Because, for most people, it's easier to connect with stories, images, and practices than with abstract truths. If you told people directly that they, themselves, are divine, limitless awareness, it likely wouldn't land very well, especially in ancient India or Jerusalem. That's why religions create symbols, rituals, commandments, and myths—ways for people to gradually move toward the truth. Words themselves, when shaped into concepts, are ways of pointing the attention of consciousness toward exploring its own nature.

We are all intellectual beings and use our minds to process the world, and different spiritual paths exist because people have different mental/intellectual capacities or levels of mind development.

For those more tied to body, emotions, or strong beliefs (beginner minds), the spiritual path is gradual, as the mind is heavily associated with the body and the physical world. Such a mind is in a pursuit of material pleasures.

For such a mind to explore spirituality, it turns to religion, which provides stories of gods, rules, and rituals. These keep attention focused, even if, at first, it's still within a world of concepts. This is the case where consciousness strongly believes in words. It lives in a world of descriptions, judgments, and evaluations. For such a type of mind, all the religious tales of gods, with detailed descriptions of their deeds and commandments, methods of worship, rituals, practices, and so forth, were created.

In fact, another "divine" world is created—in imagination. A spiritual world. But it is illusory, because though woven of loftier concepts, it still lacks direct experience. No one (sober) has ever seen gods, angels, or demons in the way they are described in scriptures. So, worldly desires, which bring nothing but suffering and dissatisfaction, are replaced with one grand desire: to know God. Or Buddha, depending on the tradition.

In imagination, opposite the thought *"I,"* the thought *"God"* is placed. And between these imagined figures, a virtual path is created, one with many stages and pathways. For this mind, the attainment of non-dual reality is very slow and riddled with obstacles. Most die before realizing their true potential. This mind will likely not find this book interesting or useful (and has probably already stopped reading two paragraphs earlier).

For the minds of intermediate capacity (intermediate minds), the path teaches transformation, as these minds are achievers, constantly setting a higher standard for themselves. Instead of rejecting emotions like anger or desire, they are used as fuel for awareness. Just like a mirror reflects anything without being changed by it, awareness can recognize all experiences as its own play.

Here, there are no deities separate from the self. Perceiving everything as one's own energies, the self becomes the deity, not separate from it. However, this is still a relative and imaginative dimension. This mind's attention is captured by the idea of transformation. There are still concepts of transforming, reincarnation, and karma. That means judgment and relative qualities remain; subject and object remain. Mirror and reflections. The sense of a "doer" or the responsible "I" remains, which is the subtlest obstacle to final realization.

Such minds may attain the non-dual spiritual realization, but the path is gradual and is through constant work and transformation. This mind may benefit from this book but will likely revolt and reject some of its teachings.

For minds with higher capacity (advanced minds), the path is direct, as the mind is pure and does not associate itself with concepts, while not rejecting them. Nothing needs to be rejected or transformed. The self is one and the same as God, the Universe, and all creation. And the distance between beginner/intermediate and this higher knowledge is like that between heaven and Earth.

Simply put: this is not knowledge based on words. The non-dual higher traditions that appeal to these minds, Advaita Vedānta and Dzogchen Buddhism, are knowledge beyond words. Beyond definitions and mental concepts. Here, there is no need to renounce anything; no need to purify or transform. This means that any manifestation arising in one's field of perception should be left as it is, without evaluating whether it is good or bad, beautiful or ugly, as one is free from all concepts and self-identifications.

In Advaita Vedānta, this is, "Prajñānam Brahma! (Consciousness is God)," "Aham Brahmasmi (I am God)." In Christianity, "I and my Father are One." In Dzogchen, "All phenomena are your mind."

This book is meant for those seeking the third level—the so-called "direct path." Although the path is direct, it requires a lot of concentration, logical reasoning, undivided attention, honesty, and earnestness. If you possess all these, please read on. If just reading this intro made you yawn, you should probably put this book away until your mind is ready to embark on this journey.

This is not to discourage you, dear reader, from continuing. Even beginner and intermediate seekers will likely find some aspects of this book useful or will spark the desire to explore spirituality further. I just want to make sure this knowledge is not forced, as it will land harmoniously only in the minds that are ready to receive it. However, the very fact that you have found this book may itself be the indication that your mind is ready and this knowledge found you at the right time.

Once you come into contact with this knowledge, you will not ever be able to remove yourself fully from it, as it will be akin to a deep recognition of finding home, and your true nature will yearn to come back to it. But if you are not fully ready to escape the delusion of duality, this book may not land well with your mind, at first.

For those joining, happy journeying!

Chapter 2

My Story of Finding this Path

ALTHOUGH THIS BOOK is meant to transcend the imagined personality and show a direct path to non-dual existence, I still chose to begin with my "personal" story of a how I found the Teaching communicated in this book. The reason I chose to include my own story is to set a context for how diverse the paths to this knowledge may be and how we turn to spirituality when we've suffered enough and the pain of continuing to live in our learned ways becomes too unbearable.

After all, if we all lived in constant harmony, peace, and happiness, what would be the point in seeking the spiritual knowledge? This path always begins with suffering or a struggle of some sort, and for some, it never ends in this lifetime. But for me and you, the lucky reader, the path ends here, as this book has everything you will need to stop searching once and for all.

Let me tell you how this Teaching found me.

1994

It's winter. Early morning, around 6:30 a.m.

I open my eyes to sounds of commotion outside. I hear people discussing something very loudly outside my window. It's 1994, and I am a six-year-old girl who lives on the first floor of a large apartment complex in the post-Soviet country of Kazakhstan. It's a concrete and brick building, and we have thick, glass windows covered with welded metal bars, as living on the first floor subjects one to the possibility of frequent break-ins.

I get up and walk outside my bedroom, through a hallway that opens up into our small kitchen. My mother is in there, making breakfast, along with my sister, who sits quietly by the window, observing the commotion outside.

I ask my mom what happened, and she says not to worry about it, to sit down and have breakfast. I love my mom and my family. Even though it's extremely tough to survive and make a decent living in the post-Soviet environment of anarchy, lawlessness, and lack of any resemblance of stability, my father manages to run several successful businesses, and my mother continues to be a wonderful homemaker, creating a comfortable and peaceful life for my sister and me.

When we leave to go to school that morning, a neighborhood friend informs us that our neighbor, Baba Vera, an old, lonely alcoholic, froze to death outside our window the night before. She left her apartment barefoot to walk to a nearby grocery store to pick up more vodka, but she fell into a pile of snow and died from freezing. The nights are usually very cold during this time of the year.

My sister and I stare at each other, our faces a mask of shock yet not surprise. Our neighborhood has seen its share of tragedies—to people we know or have seen plenty of times before.

A quiet suicide just the year before, when a neighbor leapt off their rooftop to their death and left blood stains on the sidewalk, which still remain today. Upstairs, a man who returned home with a bloody neck after being attacked and mugged while walking home. My mother, who was threatened with a knife in broad daylight outside a grocery store and only managed to escape after her gold chain was ripped off her neck.

And then there was another neighbor whose death seemed to come unexpectedly, almost abruptly. Even now, I remember the terror that came upon me when I walked past the coffin lid placed on one of the flights of stairs connecting our floors in the apartment complex…

Growing up the 1990s in a post-Soviet country is what shaped me into a tough and resilient person. We were strong, independent, and most of the time, unsupervised children, who spent most of their days away from home, either at school or playing with our friends outside. We normally only came home to eat and change.

The school we attended barely had enough desks for all students. We had no technology; blackboards had chalk that always went missing. We had ripped, used books with profanities written all over them or pages missing; and teachers who were paid so little, they could hardly care about any student's personal success.

Outside of school, there wasn't much for the kids to do—we didn't have any parks, playgrounds, or entertainment places that were geared to young adults. We would spend our afternoons hanging out at an abandoned daycare play yard that was riddled with cigarette butts and old empty beer bottles.

What I remember most from my childhood is the constant feeling of worry, of not being safe, of not quite belonging. I always questioned whether I was meant to be born in the place where I was and how I ended up there. Although religion or spirituality were never discussed or practiced in my family, I always pondered my true origins and why I was where I was.

Everything around me seemed very cold, very hostile, and very unwelcoming. I always had a feeling that this was not the actual reality of what was meant for me. I craved warmth, love, and harmony. But the world I grew up in was cold, cruel, and chaotic.

When the Soviet Union collapsed in 1991 and Kazakhstan became an independent country, my parents, along with millions of other people, lost everything overnight. Their education degrees were annulled, the factories where they worked were privatized, their social security was taken away, the currency devalued, and most of their dreams and hopes were completely shattered. This collective tragedy translated into every aspect of how people operated in the 1990s and early 2000s, while I was growing up. Everyone seemed to be angry, not trusting, bitter, financially strained, and mad at the world and themselves.

Life was tough, but we persevered. I am amazed at the strength and endurance of people who lived around me during those times. As kids, my sister and I watched VHS tapes of dubbed American movies, marveling at how structured and comfortable life could be. I dreamed of coming to this place on the screen—a place of magic, hope, laughter, and comfort, where any of your dreams could come true.

2005

I am 17, in eleventh grade, about to graduate what would be the equivalent of high school. My sister just graduated last year and is actively applying to colleges in Russia.

After the Soviet Union collapsed, it became tough for those of us who ended up in one of the post-Soviet republics outside of Russia to get a decent education, as all Soviet education was mostly centralized in Russia and its big cities. But we now are citizens of Kazakhstan, with no access to Russian schools, and the ones that are being opened locally aren't great or even accredited, since Kazakhstan is a newly independent country, trying to build its infrastructure and educational systems, along with a stable currency and economy.

Our parents know we need to move in order for us to have a chance at a better education and a better life. So, they apply for the Green Card Lottery. And win...

Despite the excitement and anticipation of what this next great chapter will bring, we are all very scared. Very, very much so. Even though life is not stable or safe, it is still *our* life—a life we are used to and have learned to love.

We have a home, friends, pets, possessions, a culture, and a language, after all! But now, we are to leave all of that behind, pack four suitcases, and travel over twenty hours to find ourselves in a foreign, completely new, and unknown to us, country, where we have nothing and know no one...

I still vividly remember the day we sold our local apartment and moved all of our things out. (Most, we sold off or donated, since we could not bring much on the plane.) We went into the apartment to pick up final items and leave the keys for the new owners.

I remember the feelings of such deep sadness and loss that came over me, as I stared at my room of ten years—completely empty, with some dust balls on the floor... I looked over at my sister, and she had tears running down her face. We both stood there, quietly crying, mourning the loss of our home and of the feeling of safety, family, and belonginess.

Ahead of us lay a great mystery of what our new life in a new country was going to be. But this empty apartment symbolized the loss of our home, the only home we knew, and one that we would never come back to. While the future held nothing but mysteries…

The feeling of losing your home like that completely tears you up from the inside. It's like mourning a death—an ending of an era of your life, with a new era not yet beginning, one that carries many unknowns and fears.

Homes are important to people. We need the feelings of safety, belonginess, warmth, and familiarity. We are creatures of habit and are naturally resistant to change, even fearful of it. We cling to what is familiar, and we fear the unknown. Even if that unknown carries a lot of potential for a better life, we still cling to the past, afraid to embrace the unfamiliar. We live in a dim room that we know by heart. We know where the furniture is, where the sharp corners are, and which floorboards creak.

The door to the next room is open, and light spills in from it, but stepping through the door will mean not knowing where the walls are yet. Even when the next room is brighter, we often stay in the dark, not because it is better, but because it is familiar.

Being torn away from home, even if it was just a dark room, comes with fear, sadness, and a profound sense of loss. When we lost that apartment to go chase the American Dream, the sense of loss completely consumed me, leaving a deep scar in my memory of what home once was…

Thinking back to that time, I am always amazed at how strong and resilient human beings really are. My family made it work. My college-educated engineer parents got jobs cleaning homes; my sister and I went to a local community college and started our educational pursuits while working in retail and service part-time. We lived in a tiny apartment, had one car, and could not afford much above food and basic necessities.

The first few years of living in this brand-new reality put a lot of stress on our family. We fought and cried a lot, with many occasional, "I wish we'd never moved…"

This immigration was the first traumatic experience of my adult life—a true death and rebirth of sorts, where the old self was completely replaced by a brand new one. And that replacement was a painful, stressful, long, and cruel process. A familiar home was replaced by a new, temporary one, where everything was unfamiliar and scary.

That was when I learned that life was tough, and one needed to constantly overcome as a basic way of existence. Constantly strive forward, achieve, attain, and suffer through change—all in the name of transformation and creating a better life; all in the name of some ethereal "success," a pursuit of happiness. A sense of loss remained, however, buried deep inside all four of us, but we needed to move on, to keep building a new life, a new home, a new version of our family, and a story of our American Dream, where resilience and perseverance bring success and a better life.

Our family relationships deteriorated greatly during this time. We all suppressed our fear, anger, and sadness, and we were afraid to talk about any of it, while the distance between us grew rapidly. My sister and I would leave every morning to go to school and then to work, and my parents did the same. Each one of us plugged along, kept our heads down, and just wanted to make it through the day.

Because of the language barrier and the fact that we were new to the area, we did not have any friends or other people we could confide in. The rare times when we ate dinner together, we sat in silence or exchanged a few words about how our days went. More often, we would fight.

The fights would break out for no apparent reason, but they always stemmed from one of us letting their frustration out, and the others chiming in with how their frustration was more important or more justified. Each one of us felt like we carried the weight of the world on our shoulders, so when someone else voiced their own struggles and pains, we argued over whose struggles were harder or more important and who had more reasons to be tired and angry.

As sad as I am to admit it, we had nothing but a clash of egos going on at that time, where each one of us felt overlooked, pushed aside, and not recognized for their pain and struggles. In reality, we all struggled greatly. Hard times were putting a severe strain on our relationships, and instead of being there for one another, we each retreated further back into our respective corners, where our egos built walls of pain and resentment around each one of us.

These times were the toughest. I avoided my parents, as each interaction almost always ended up in a fight. I felt alone and unprotected. I felt like my parents stopped loving me and were always looking for a reason to blame any of their shortcomings on me. My father, whom I idolized and adored as a child, became a distant and mean man whom I felt I did not know at all.

Each time I attempted to have a conversation with him, it ended in a screaming match, after which we did not speak for weeks or months. Because we spent very little time at home, it was easy to avoid him, and I just kept working and going to school in hopes of becoming successful on my own, moving out, and building a better life for my sister and me.

2008

Equipped with this drive to succeed and with my natural intelligence, I overcame, achieved, and attained, until I found myself graduating college, moving out of my parents' house, finding a good job, and then going to and finishing law school, all while working fulltime and having no quantifiable "joy" from my achievements.

I remember the feeling of longing or anticipation of something… something ethereal and vague that sat, dim, on the never-reachable horizon. That feeling of "how I will feel when I finally achieve this." And yet never quite reaching that horizon or feeling that feeling, because the horizon always shifted further away as I grew closer.

Then, more goals were added—graduate, get a job, make money, pay off student loans, get married, have kids, build a career and influence, become rich… And then… That "then" was never something I understood, as I struggled to grasp exactly when that feeling of satisfaction, happiness, and pure content would come to me. After all the above were attained? Or somewhere in between?

But somehow, I knew exactly what that would feel like. I could visualize and "taste" it—the feeling of complete peace, harmony, and pure love and contentment for all. I realize now that we don't chase goals; we chase the state of being that attaining them will bring to us. Back then, none of my materialistic goals quite brought me there.

I attributed this lack of satisfaction and contentment to my inherent nature as a hopeless perfectionist and romantic. We are all born with different minds, and we are shaped by our environments to perceive this reality in our own unique, individual way. As an individual, I always wanted everything to be at the highest possible level. If I go to school, I can only be top of my class. If I get a job, it should be the best job that only the top one percent of graduates get. If I exercise or set a physical goal, I can literally stop eating and sleeping until I perfect that goal.

And when it came to romantic relationships, boy oh boy, did I have an expectation… Nothing short of a prince in shining armor riding into my life on his white horse and chasing all my troubles away with his love and care. I didn't date until I was almost twenty years old, because of my super-high expectations, my unwillingness to settle for less, and my unshakeable idea that a prince would come after all, when the time was right. I could not waste my time on other romantic experiences while awaiting *him*. Granted, I scared away a lot of potential pursuers with this attitude.

But one stuck around. We met online and connected over our shared culture, language, and backgrounds. He was also a recent immigrant who worked three jobs, supported his mother, and studied for the exam to get into dental school. He made me feel that familiar sense of home, as someone to whom I could talk to freely about all sorts of things, most of which we had in common. He was someone who had my same drive for success and spirit for achieving and persevering. At first, I was not romantically interested, and I made myself very clear. But he persevered and kept pursuing until I gave in and fell deeply in love.

When he moved away for dental school and decided not to come back, my world collapsed. I had my law school admission letters, along with a nice scholarship in addition to in-state tuition paid, but I could not feel that quantifiable joy I was craving from any of these achievements. At that time, my ethereal "then" was tied to him—a feeling I would have, once we reconnected and stayed happily ever after. A chasing of a dream again, a constant longing for a feeling of peace, contentment, and complete satisfaction.

Academic or career achievements meant nothing to me at that point, as my ego shifted to pursue another ethereal "then" goal—one of building a family and a home with a man I loved.

2011

I deferred my law school admission, quit my job, packed up my things, and moved to Colorado. I showed up at his door, told him I'd left everything behind, and then started my life anew yet again. I found a job, applied and got into law schools in Colorado, got married, and began building a new "then" with the man I thought I would spend the rest of my life with.

Was I fully content, peaceful, and satisfied, now that I had what I wanted yet again? No. That feeling of not quite being there yet still remained.

Now, I realize that the ego never stops searching; it is never content or fully happy, as the struggle toward and the achievement of the next goal is what it lives off. And sadly, the people who persevere and achieve the most are usually the most troubled and unhappy, internally. The bigger the ego, the bigger the successes and achievements, then the bigger void at the lack of satisfaction, and the constant rat race to achieve more. The rat race for the state of feeling content, harmonious, and still. But sadly, for most of these people, those feelings never come, and they die chasing the next "then," in hopes of attaining harmony after all.

I was not happy in my marriage. I constantly felt alone, unheard, and unappreciated. I voiced my frustrations, and the fights ensued, followed by weeks and months of not speaking, each one of us again retreating into the corners behind the walls our egos built around us.

He felt the same—alone, unloved, unheard. Two strong personalities, immigrant overachievers, who focused on setting goals, attaining them, and moving to the next ones, we lived in a clash of two egos yet again. What I ran away from when I left my parents' house once again flourished in my marriage.

Now I understand that you can never run away from your ego—when you seek comfort and approval from others, you are bound for failure. All our lives, we feel our parents wronged us by not loving us properly; our teachers failed us by not paying enough attention to us among thirty other kids; our employers fail us by not recognizing our talents; and our spouses/significant others fail us by not giving up their own needs in our favor. The ego cycle remains unbroken for those who are used to living in this social dynamic of self-approval via others, and that's how 99% of people live.

2015-2019

In the rare times when my husband and I got along or made up after a fight, we still clung to each other, cherishing the connections and similarities that initially drew us to each other, while looking for ways to make it last. And that's when one more common goal united us again: the goal of becoming parents.

Children are also huge ego boosters. A helpless being who depends on us for everything, to whom we become the center of the universe—that's a major way for the ego to confirm its importance for others. The love we feel for our children is pure at first, but it gets muddied by the ego. As the child grows and starts disagreeing with us or challenging us, we begin withdrawing love as punishment for such disagreements or challenges, and we reward with love when they comply or agree with us.

I had my first son in 2015, followed by my second son in 2016, and my daughter in 2019, all born in the glimpses of happiness my husband and I had found in between the ego wars; all born out of the underlying pure love and hope for harmony and happiness; all deeply loved and cherished as a start of a new era, one where our family could be united and happy.

The experience of motherhood was my first awakening to the concept of pure, unconditional love. I started feeling these outbursts of pure joy and happiness for no reason, just by being around my babies. Tiredness, lack of sleep, problems in my marriage—all faded when I was enjoying the day-to-day of loving and caring for the new humans I had made. I began to truly get glimpses of what it meant to love unconditionally, as my children were growing up and misbehaving or challenging me. I simply could not imagine loving them any less for acting a certain way.

My family and those close to me said I was too soft as a parent, that I should have had rules and boundaries, and that such lax parenting was going to bite me in the you-know-what eventually, when my kids grew up. But I simply could not be a different mother; to me, there were no boundaries or rules to impose into the love I felt for them. That was my first glimpse into our true nondual nature.

My marriage did not get better, though. I just found an outlet to direct my energy toward and didn't have much left for fighting. But we continued growing further apart, now that I was even more distant than before, with my world revolving around the kids and his around his work. Seemingly, we had everything any young family would want or need: we were young, healthy, educated, and successful, with three beautiful, healthy kids.

Every attempt to communicate or grow closer again ended up in fights and wounded egos, where we both felt unheard and uncared for. I wanted support and help with raising the kids while trying to build a new law firm, while he wanted a more present, caring wife who prioritized the marital relationship as much as the children. After each screaming match, we would retreat to our corners to lick our wounds and wallow in our own self-righteousness and self-pity.

Now I know this is exactly how the ego thrives—by contrasting against the other and prioritizing the self over hearing the other and finding common ground. But back then, I felt completely broken, unheard, unloved, and abandoned. The overachiever in me flourished. Now I was also a mother who had to persevere and prove to my husband and the entire world that I could be a successful business owner while taking care of three young children.

My ego struggled, persevered, and attained—all fueled by the self-righteousness and the blame I kept placing on my husband for being a bad irresponsible father, for abandoning me in my parental duties, and for not being fully present during this important formative time for our family. He felt my anger and frustration with him, but his ego also did not allow him to take the first step toward finding a common ground. His way of showing up was providing us with financial well-being, and each time we made up, he tried to diffuse my frustration by buying me a present or moving us to a bigger house.

There were times when we wouldn't speak for weeks, as the new big house only expanded the distance between us, where we didn't have to see each other even while living under the same roof. My frustration with him not being there for me and the kids most of the time grew larger, and he became more and more distant and avoided me in fear of another loud fight.

When I first filed for divorce, he suggested therapy, but that failed miserably for us, as therapy only adds fuel to the ego-fire by assigning blame and digging though past traumas to explain one's shortcomings. The longer you do therapy, the more the ego flourishes and finds excuses by assigning blame to parents, teachers, spouses, a kid from kindergarten who pushed you off the swing, an angry school bus driver who made you feel scared, etc., etc.

2022

When therapy failed, he filed for divorce this time. I remember the day I got served. I was in the office and spent the whole day in shock. But when I got home, the finality of it hit me like a train going full speed, completely crushing me. I collapsed on the stairs and wailed until I couldn't breathe, with one thought circulating in my mind: *This is the end, this is the end, this is the end...*

The ensuing months are a bit foggy, as I was constantly in a dream-like state—being awake and present but not quite on track with reality. I couldn't sleep; I barely ate; I had wine every night; and I cried so much, I thought I would lose my eyesight. Divorce is like a death; even if it was a long time coming, it still feels very raw, very final, and very lonely. The person you once thought was your lifetime partner is now a stranger whom you communicate with through court filings.

The day I moved out of our family home with the kids was another big death—just like I'd experienced in my childhood apartment in Kazakhstan. A feeling of loss, of an ending, of deep painful sadness, where you see your home being stripped down to the walls, but you can still vividly remember your kids' laughter and the smell of the family dinner echoing in its empty rooms... It felt like part of me died with the loss of my home and the memories that had been created there.

Losing my marriage ignited a new fire of overachieving in me, as I no longer had another provider to rely on. I had no time to wallow in my self-pity or process the loss. At this point, I had to make my firm be an actual stable income stream, so I would not have to rely on child support or constantly ask for a handout from my ex-husband.

My ego was fully ready to go out and conquer and achieve to prove to the world and to him that I could be single, yet successful and self-sufficient. And I made it happen. Month by month, year after year, my firm continued growing. I hired more employees; I started making enough to sustain myself and my kids, even if my ex-husband stopped helping financially.

All of these accomplishments, though, did not bring any feelings of deep satisfaction or peace and contentment yet again, as I felt like the deeper inner harmony I so desperately wanted was an ethereal, unrealistic dream at this point. It seemed, no matter what I did—like ended an unhappy relationship, achieved new financials goals, traveled, or grew my business—I still was not fully satisfied with the outcome.

At times, I doubted the divorce; I kept thinking we should have persevered and saved our marriage for the sake of our kids. I kept picturing a life where we were still together and how different it would have been for us and the children. At other times, different thoughts consumed me, and I was actually grateful for the divorce and the new opportunities for growth that it had brought me.

Ad astra per aspera[1] was my moto and the sad story of my life. Success and achievement always came through hardship; not just to me, but it seemed to be a common theme to many stories of success I heard from clients, saw in movies, or read about in books. A human path seems to be one laid with many obstacles that one has to overcome in order to achieve and grow. To me, though, it seemed like there had to be a way to live happily and in harmony without having to ride the eternal rollercoaster loop from failure to success and back.

---

1 "To the stars through hardships," Latin.

All of my achievements also took place during the time when I was still very deep in my internal grief for the death of my marriage. Although I concealed it masterfully, deep inside I was raw and broken for years, mourning the loss of a man whom I had considered to be my life partner. Eventually, I learned to live with that grief, and I distracted myself from it by working hard and achieving, by being the best mother I could possibly be, by travelling, by shopping, and exercising, etc. But the dull pain and the constant feeling like a part of me had died and I would never be able to take a full breath again remained. I craved inner peace and harmony.

Turn to Spirituality

It's funny how people only truly turn to spirituality when they have hit rock bottom. By "truly" I mean making it their number-one priority, not just explorations of different philosophies and the occasional visits to a temple of some sort.

I always explored spirituality not as a number-one priority, but as a search for the ultimate truth, a longing for a "home" of some sort, where all puzzle pieces would finally fit into place and true inner peace of resting in the knowledge of one's true actual nature would follow. As I briefly stated in the introduction, I researched world religions (not just the theological books, but also historic research on the origins of all religions). I followed various spiritual influencers, read multiple books, attended retreats, and practiced yoga and meditation. I learned so much; too much to actually piece out any coherent ultimate answers from. I would follow one teaching but then find faults in it and move on to the other, only to overanalyze and get disappointed again. I was never a full adept of just one teaching or religion, as none of them ever actually gave me complete answers as to the ultimate truth and nature of God.

The true turn to spirituality for me only occurred after my second "death"—the excruciatingly painful divorce that I described above. At that point, I was so emotionally drained and in such constant pain, finding a way to inner peace became my number-one priority. I had to continue living for myself and my kids, but I could not physically tolerate living in constant suffering or the fear of suffering during the brief glimpses of happiness. My one and only objective in life became attaining inner peace. And I knew, to find it, I would have to find God.

I won't recount every step of the way, as the only important step worth mentioning gave birth to this book and is the ultimate step I took to end the constant samsara cycle of pain-pleasure. The methods and ways I found and tried all gave temporary relief—a bit longer of a period of pleasure—but they all still ended up in pain. (When I say "pain," it's not just to indicate the actual pain or suffering, but rather a whole slew of negative emotions like doubt, worry, inner conflict, restlessness, etc.)

When religions were explored and set aside as the "opium for the masses,"[2] I started with ayahuasca ceremonies, which gave a temporary glimpse into pure pleasure of our true self (Sat Chit Ananda, which will be discussed in detail in this book), but eventually the effect fizzled out. The facilitators would just tell me that I needed to "integrate" my experiences or go to more ceremonies to

---

[2] Karl Marx.

dig deeper. I then turned to hypnosis and past-life regressions, during which I again received a lot of insights and glimpses into peace, but the effects were also temporary and required more and more work. The cycle of pain and pleasure went on.

I then started following and practicing teachings of a few famous modern-day New Age spiritual leaders, whose names I won't mention here for ethical reasons. These gave me greater insights and actually correlated with our modern-day realities a lot more than the ancient religious dogmas, but I still did not feel like suffering could end once and for all.

Just like traditional therapy/psychology, all of these teachings create a never-ending path—a path of a seeker who constantly searches, finds, analyzes, improves, moves on, and continues searching. The master comes up with a new course, a new book, or a new aspect that needs to be worked on, and the followers keep buying the next shiny object. These paths are gradual and never seem to actually reach a point of a finality of some sort—when one completely sheds suffering and lives in bliss and peace.

This is similar to major world religions—a path to God in them is just a path of constant self-improvement, and true completeness does not occur in our human lives. With some of these modern teachings, this complete realization or the end of the path would only come after death; in others, it would occur if you completely renounced your worldly life and spent decades in meditation. Neither appeared like a good option to me, as I kept feeling like there had to be a way to attain peace and reach the end of the path while still living my human life. My constant hunger for true inner peace kept driving me to look for more.

And then, one day, I found Him—my Teacher, my Savior, a precious guru I will forever cherish and praise, Pasha Narasimha. I saw a clip of his podcast on social media and followed to his Telegram channel, which was titled "One who does not exist." Intrigued, I joined the channel and started watching and reading his content, amazed and angered at the same time, as everything he was saying revolved around one idea: "You do not exist. Accept this, and life will be pure bliss."

> *Everything you consider so important—all your beliefs, rituals, customs, and rites. Everything you accept and reject, condemn and praise; all meanings and goals; control over your life and free will; religions and spiritual practices; personal growth and ideas of development; psychology and psychoanalysis; politics and relations between men and women; petty little problems, sighs and groans, nipples, penises, and butterflies in the stomach, as well as all your notions of God, the soul, heaven, hell, angels, demons, and other abstract concepts, including scientific and historical descriptions of the world, ALL OF THIS and much, much more, is real for you only because you BELIEVE in yourselves as separate I-entities, distinct from one another.*
>
> *When, as a result of self-inquiry, you discover that the character you took yourself to be does not actually exist-that it is nothing more than a virtual hologram, a fantasy of your imagination made of an insubstantial, dreamlike substance, YOUR ENTIRE INVENTED LITTLE WORLD immediately collapses like a house of cards. And along with it, all*

> *your naïve "values," to which you obsessively attribute reality, are irrevocably exposed as illusions.*
>
> *From that moment on, the human world appears to you like an amusing cartoon that no longer holds any importance for you. You find yourself as the only existing, eternal, immortal, and absolutely perfect CONSCIOUSNESS, originally free from any limitations whatsoever. You discover yourself to be GOD.*
>
> —Pasha Narasimha
> (translated from Russian by the author)

I joined some of Pasha's Zoom meetings that were open to everyone who wanted to explore his Teaching and was considering joining the three-day program. During the meetings, I realized that Pasha was teaching a modern, easy-to-digest Advaita Vedānta or Dzogchen Buddhism—some of which I'd explored on my spiritual quest but failed to fully grasp or understand. Truly, the ancient non-dual teachings are very hard to understand, as translations from Sanskrit and the intricacy of language make them all appear like Shakespear writings—beautiful, creative, but hard to follow, and having more of a poetic nature than a practical one. I used to read them, even with commentary, but I never truly understood the practical applications of the words. What Pasha was teaching, however, was easy to follow, and I was so intrigued and excited that I'd found a modern teacher who could "speak" Advaita in simple and understandable terms!

I joined Pasha's three-day program in April 2024, when I was thirty-six years old, and that was the time when the "I" I had lived with all my life died. But this death was also a birth of a new era—one of knowing myself as God, pure consciousness, the Universe (whatever word describes the absolute); one where suffering is not possible, and one where my longing for internal peace and harmony is finally fulfilled and will never be disturbed in all eternity.

I know these are big words, but they truly describe the state I was able to achieve after living and breathing the Teaching of Pasha for over a year and a half. The Teaching gave birth to this book, as sharing this Teaching, this profound spiritual knowledge, became my absolute priority after I realized it for myself. This Teaching does not belong to anyone, but it should be known to all; yet it is also not something that can be easily shared in casual conversations with my friends or family. That's why I spent time living the Teaching and then writing it in my own words, but staying very true to what Pasha has taught me.

I already warned in the Introduction that this Teaching is not for everyone. I want to reiterate it here, but not to discourage anyone from reading on; just to state that once you come in contact with this Teaching, your life will completely change. Your true self will recognize the Truth, and there will be an immediate reaction of finding home. But to truly integrate it, a lot of effort will be required.

Your ego will revolt; you will feel exhausted after reading just a few pages of some sections, and you will have serious internal conflict and drama before fully integrating this into "your" life. I put quotation marks around "your," as after fully integrating this teaching, your "I" will die just like mine did, and no sense of possession will ever exist again. So, if "you" are ready to die and never come back to suffering, please read on, but only if you can make this

Teaching your number-one priority until you fully integrate it.

Enlightenment: What It Means and How It Applies to this Teaching.

Before we begin the journey of the rational exploration of our ultimate nature and become free of suffering, it is important to understand how the process of becoming "enlightened" actually works.

Typically, when we think of enlightenment, we imagine a monk or a saint or a guru of some sort who has experienced some spiritually dramatic event (an "awakening") after years of spiritual practice, isolation, mediation, or by virtue of receiving a message/revelation of the ultimate truth from a spiritual power (an angel, God, etc.). Such an enlightened person, we imagine, is detached from the worldly activities, emotions, and feelings, and they walk around with a blissful smile of complete acceptance, contentment, and universal love for every living creature. (He may also have a halo around his head and consume heavenly manna instead of food.)

In the real and practical sense, though, enlightenment is not some magical revelation but is a process of shining the light of awareness on every aspect of our nature. We use the light of awareness to scan (like an X-ray) each and every part of our existence. Enlightenment is just deep and attentive self-exploration, and when we explore our every aspect and confirm certain facts we find in the process through our actual experience, we can attain the peace of knowing (not believing!) everything about our ultimate nature.

This is how I want you to approach the Teaching—using your own awareness, reason, and five senses to confirm everything that will be covered below through your own practical experience. There will be concepts that will rattle you or cause your mind to throw a tantrum and protest, but if you retreat to the conscious and rational awareness, you will succeed on this journey of becoming enlightened in the most rational and practical sense of the word.

Chapter 3

Concept 1 of the Teaching: Space/Consciousness

"Spirituality is just science we don't understand. Yet."
~Quote from *12 Monkeys*

Where Does God Exist?

WHAT WE USUALLY are taught in any major religions appealing to the first type of human minds (beginner minds) is that there exists a God who created our world and has the power to fix or destroy it, punish or reward its inhabitants, and perform any other actions as an onlooker. This concept never sat well with me, as I have a hard time imagining where and how this God could exist, if everything in the Universe exists in the same space.

If you start an imaginary line from your finger and extend it beyond all physical objects, then outside the planet, then into multiple galaxies, stars, etc., would that line ever end? The answer is logically No, as how can space or nothingness around all objects ever run out? Plus, all that is known to science is that everything is made of the same underlying particles that shape up into energies that then create physical objects. If we remove the limitations of human vision and look at the world with the strongest microscope, or these days even a quantum particle viewer, everything appears as one matter. That matter itself is space or emptiness/nothingness, in which all known phenomena appear—planets, stars, shapes, people, animals, thoughts, dreams, etc.

Where, then, can this separate God exist? Can there be another space outside of the only space we know, where everything exists?

Thus, true spirituality to me goes hand in hand with science and its developments, which modern quantum physics perfectly demonstrates. The quote I chose as the opening for this section ("Spirituality is just science we don't understand. Yet.") finds profound expression in the meeting point between quantum physics and the ancient teachings of Advaita Vedānta and Dzogchen—the highest non-dual traditions in Hinduism and Buddhism.

Both traditions assert that all distinctions—between subject and object, self and other—are illusions arising within one indivisible consciousness. Similarly, modern quantum theory reveals that the apparent solidity and separation of the world dissolve at the subatomic level into an infinite field of potentialities. Particles exist not as independent entities but as probabilities within a unified quantum field, which manifests as form only through observation—an echo of the Vedantic and Dzogchen view that reality arises through awareness itself. Thus, what the sages called Brahman (ultimate all-pervading reality) or the Dharmakaya (the true body of Buddha is nothingness/void), science now glimpses as the quantum vacuum: the boundless source from which all phenomena emerge and into which they return, unbroken and whole.

Yet the concept of God in most mainstream religions I studied, before discovering Advaita or Dzogchen, represents God as something that exists outside of us—in some unreachable-to-us dimension, where we can only find ourselves after death, if we lead a virtuous enough life. But for this Godly dimension (or Heaven) to exist, it needs to exist in some space.

Quantum physics tells us that the quantum field is the living void within which all things appear. That is the space that has no boundaries and is infinite—this nothingness or void. So how can there truly be a space/void where God's dimension exists, inside or outside this already infinite and all-pervading void? Such a notion collapses into paradox, for the void has no boundaries, no inside or outside. What we call God may then, logically, arise only in this same infinite void—within the one undivided field.

In truth, everything—observer and observed alike—is woven from the same subtle essence, the same luminous emptiness. This void is not dead or inert; it is conscious. It knows itself through the dance of forms it gives rise to. God, then, is not a separate being within this field but the field itself, the silent awareness in which all perception unfolds.

Think about it with your eyes closed. When you see no physical boundaries yet are aware of the space you exist in—the space between the particles in your brain is the same space between the particles of every other mind, and the same space within the atoms of every mountain, star, and breath of air. There is only one void where all of these particles exist, infinite and awake, appearing as the universe and all that seems to be.

Ask yourself, could there be anything before this space/void? How can there be a void beyond a void, a before before the void appeared? It is logically impossible. The space/void never appeared, never disappeared, and it exists independently of and unaffected by anything that appears and disappears in it.

Thus, the first concept of the Teaching is about using the light of your awareness to rationally confirm that everything we know, feel, see, and perceive appears in one space. This space has no beginning and no end, and within this space/nothingness, everything appears, lasts, and disappears. Yet this space/nothingness is not so simple as just empty and dead. It has potential for things to appear and disappear in it—a certain power of manifesting things/shapes/concepts/all known phenomena to appear, to last, and to disappear in this constant space that has no boundaries and no beginning or end.

It has one more characteristic that we can discover when we close our eyes: it is capable of awareness. Somehow, when there are no forms, concepts, energies, or anything to perceive, the perception or awareness is still there.

Close your eyes again, and realize this: when there is nothing that is perceived, the perceiver is still aware—aware of this emptiness/nothingness. When things, concepts, or shapes appear, it becomes aware of them, as well, but this awareness is not tied to anything; it exists beyond and independent of anything that appears in it. Thus, by using the light of our reasoning, we see that everything exists in one void/space, and this void is aware of everything that exists in it.

As mentioned before, all religious traditions express this concept in the way of using the Holy Triad. Using the Hindu tradition, think of it like this: for the world (including your body and mind) to appear, there must first be open space—that's Shiva. For anything to actually arise, there has to be potential, like a tree inside a seed—that's Brahman.

And then there's the ability to notice and experience it all—that's Vishnu. In Advaita Vedanta, the luminous self-aware space of the origin is called Sat Chit Ananda—Existence/Being, Consciousness, Bliss. Again, three characteristics of the original self/God.

So, you see, the concepts of the Holy Trinity are nothing but the characteristics of one common space in which we all exist. One space that has the potential of manifesting anything and is aware of everything it manifests. God is this space/void—the original, never-beginning, never-ending, boundlessly aware space. In scientific terms, it's the bountiful quantum field that has absolute potential to create anything by its own awareness. But in order to explain the quantum theory to beginner minds, the concepts of the Holy Trinity were created.

The way my Teacher Pasha explained this is this: space has no borders, no center, no edges. It is infinite. Even when we try to imagine limits, those limits must appear in something—and that something is still space itself. There is nowhere outside of it for a boundary to be placed.

Because space is infinite, it is also without beginning. There is nothing it could have emerged from, no prior container, no "other" space from which it could have been separated. There has never been a moment when space was not.

Think about it using your own enlightenment—could the void appear at some point? And if so, where would it appear out of? Another void? You arrive at a paradox once again, leading to a logical conclusion that space/void always was, is, and will be.

That which is infinite and without beginning is, by definition, immortal. Space cannot disappear. There is nowhere for emptiness to go, nothing that could destroy it, and no force outside of it that could act upon it, because there is only space.

Space is not a mathematical zero or a dead absence. It is something that is directly known, directly experienced. And from it, everything we call matter appears, unfolds, and takes shape as its immediate continuation. Living beings appear out of this space/void, which logically means that space is alive (or how can something that is dead give rise to something that is living?). This is called Śakti (living energy) in Advaita Vedānta. Nothing manifests without Śakti. Space without Śakti would be inert, but in Vedānta, space is never inert, as logically follows from my statement.

If at some point—at a random moment in the middle of eternity—something appeared from emptiness, that means emptiness contained the absolute potential to become anything. Emptiness, then, is not lack but fullness. Forms cannot exist without space; they are temporary expressions of it. Space is primary. Matter is secondary. But they are one, as matter cannot exist outside of space.

Even the smallest particle of matter, the quark, is not something separate from space. It is, more accurately, a tension, a density, a disturbance within space itself. A wave does not float on top of the ocean; it is the ocean appearing as movement. In the same way, matter is not located in space; it is space momentarily condensed. This means there is no true distance between objects, just as there is no distance between what is perceived and what perceives it. There are no independent, self-existing things. What exists is one seamless, indivisible reality.

Advaita Vedānta echoes this: in it, reality is described as a single breath moving through countless openings. Each opening believes it is breathing on its own, yet the air was never divided, never owned, never localized. When one opening closes, the breath does not disappear; it simply continues without form. What seemed separate was only the breath momentarily shaped by an opening. There were never many breaths, only one moving as many.

To demonstrate this through a practical story, think about it this way:

There once was a child who loved building castles out of sand. Every day, she would come to the shore and spend hours shaping towers, walls, and little windows with careful attention. Some days, the castles were strong and tall. Other days, the tide would come early and wash them away.

One afternoon, she asked her father, "Why does everything I build disappear?"

Her father smiled and said, "Look closer."

She paused, confused, and looked at the castle in front of her.

"What do you see?" he asked.

"A castle," she said.

"And what is it made of?"

"Sand."

"And before it was a castle?"

"...just sand."

"And after the wave takes it?"

"...sand again."

The child was quiet for a moment.

"So, the castle isn't really something separate from sand?" she asked.

Her father shook his head gently. "It's sand, taking shape for a little while."

The next day, they came earlier, before anyone else had arrived. The beach was completely smooth and untouched.

"No castles," she said.

"No castles," her father agreed. "But is the sand gone?"

She looked down at the vast shoreline stretching in every direction.

"No... It's all still here."

"Exactly," he said. "The sand doesn't need the castle to exist. But the castle cannot exist without the sand."

In the same way, what we call "space" is like that sand. At times, it appears as forms—bodies, objects, thoughts, entire worlds. At other times, it seems empty, like a smooth, untouched beach. But the "emptiness" is not nothing. It is the same substance, before it takes shape.

And just as sand becomes castles without ever becoming something else, space becomes matter—living, moving, breathing—without ever ceasing to be itself. In Advaita, this living capacity of space to become form is called Śakti. It is not something added to space. It is space itself... expressing. So, nothing truly comes "out of nothing." What appears as form is simply the fullness of space, briefly taking shape—and then returning to itself again.

A human being is also a condensation of space. The space "inside" the head and the space "outside" the body are not two different spaces. They are the same. Awareness is not localized in the brain; it is equal to space itself. Fat tissue, neurons, or electrical impulses do not know the world. They are not aware of anything. They themselves are objects of perception—material that can be observed in a laboratory. The eyes do not see; they are simply the medium through which seeing happens. Space is aware of itself and its manifestations through countless forms and tools, such as eyes, brain, skin, etc.

Over the course of a lifetime, the body completely replaces itself at the cellular level many times over. There is no stable, permanent "person" underneath this process. A name is simply a label applied to trillions of endlessly changing cells, to a body that is never the same from one moment to the next. What remains constant is not the form, but the space that is aware. (This will be discussed further in the following chapter; for now, it is important to grasp that we appear in one unified field of space, live in it, and disappear into it.)

This holiday break, I visited the Kennedy Space Center in Florida with my kids. We sat down to watch their IMAX movie, *Deep Sky*, about space and the use of the NASA's Webb telescope to gather information and images about ancient galaxies and recently discovered planets that may contain life. Watching *Deep Sky* felt like confirmation of everything I have learned from Pasha, Advaita, and Dzogchen.

The telescope does not simply look outward into distant galaxies; it looks backward into the origins of form itself, revealing vast fields of darkness punctuated by quiet bursts of light. The telescope finds ancient galaxies that were formed by the Big Bang, which I see as clarity appearing without effort from an open expanse that was never inert or void. The Big Bang itself was God manifesting itself as form. In Advaita terms, it is Brahman appearing as form while never leaving its own formlessness. Space is not empty. It is alive with potential, and form is nothing but its temporary shimmer.

What resonated with me and the ideas in this book most about *Deep Sky* was one of the recurring reflections among scientists studying the deep universe, which is the realization that the elements forming those distant galaxies—the hydrogen, carbon, calcium, and heavier elements forged in ancient stars—are the very same elements that make up our bodies.

As Carl Sagan once put it, "We are made of star stuff."

This is not poetry layered onto science; it is a literal statement of continuity. There is no fundamental separation between the one who looks and what is being seen. The same space that gives birth to galaxies gives rise to thought, breath, and awareness itself. From this view, consciousness is not an accident occurring inside matter; matter is a patterned expression arising within consciousness.

Deep Sky becomes a modern mirror of the ancient insight: what appears infinitely far away is not other; it is the same luminous field, knowing itself from different points of view, where everything is made out of the same particles. Distance, time, and measurements are all just concepts we operate from this point of observation, but they do not exist in the vast absolute space of who we truly are.

In conclusion, in this section we have enlightened the following: Space is infinite, without beginning, immortal, has absolute potential, and is aware. The description of God in all monotheistic religions—beginningless, eternal, indestructible, omnipresent, all-encompassing, all-seeing, and all-powerful—matches these properties exactly.

- ✧ Space is God. And there is only that.
- ✧ The Holy Trinity is the main characteristic of this Space/God.

- ✧ What is perceived, what perceives, and the very act of perceiving are not three separate things.
- ✧ Space is absolute potential.
- ✧ Absolute potential is consciousness.
- ✧ Consciousness appears as form.
- ✧ Space, absolute potential, and consciousness are three aspects of One.

Where Does "I" Exist?

Now that we have concluded that space is one and there can be no God outside of this space, where do we find our own selves? Where does "I" exist?

We all live with a sense of individuality, separateness from one another. We see ourselves as individual personalities that are separate from one another, have relationships with one another, and can love and hate those separate-from-us beings. We have an ego—a self that possesses certain characteristics distinct from others, vices and virtues, accomplishments and failures, karmic depositories of energies, even past lives or an individual soul.

But let's use the magic light of our awareness again to enlighten the concept of this ego-self. Where does it exist? Going back to our discussion above, we are all built out of the same particles that exist in one unified space/void. On the quantum level, all our bodies are the same—a vibration of these quantum particles organized in cells, organs, fluids, neurons, etc. Examining ten people under one quantum microscope will make them look like one unified field with no boundaries between each body.

Knowing that, on the foundational level, we are all one, where does the individual "I" come from? My Teacher Pasha gave us a great example to illustrate.

He was once invited to conduct an informal couples' therapy session for his friends, John and Mary. John and Mary had been married for many years, had children, assets, and all the usual stuff. And, like many couples, they had been experiencing difficulties in their marriage, where they had disagreements, arguments, and lots of conflict.

When they sat down with the Teacher, he asked them to voice their concerns. Mary began by rattling off a list of issues she found in the way John conducted himself in their marriage—his laziness, lack of attention, even a tendency to lie. She concluded with the statement that she wanted to divorce John.

The Teacher asked Mary whom specifically she was divorcing. Looking puzzled, Mary stated, "Him," and pointed toward her husband.

"His body, then?" asked the Teacher.

"No, don't be ridiculous. Him, the person. John!" Mary exclaimed.

"My dear, John is just a name, and what you are pointing to is just a body. So, let's discern whom this being you are divorcing truly is," replied the Teacher. "Is it the skin, fat, hair, blood, internal organs, and maybe his brain?"

Mary was getting agitated. "No, it's not his biological structures, of course!"

"Then what is it? What do you call *John*? Who harmed you, if it wasn't this biological structure?"

"No, it's all of him—his personality, his thoughts, his actions."

"So, John is thoughts and actions?"

"No! He is the one who thinks the thoughts and does the actions!" exclaimed Mary, angrily.

"You are giving me labels that describe his characteristics, but where is John who owns or creates these words, thoughts, or actions? Where does he exist? We just determined he is not the name, the body, or the thoughts or actions, so where is John who acts, thinks, and has a personality?" the Teacher insisted.

Mary was, as you, too, probably are now, at a loss.

Let's think this through as it relates to our own selves. When you say "I," what do you actually mean? Is it your name, your body, your thoughts, your actions? Those all describe you, but are they *you*?

You may say, "I am a combination of all this," but "combination" is also just a word, a description that does not tell anyone who you truly are. To put it differently, who possesses this combination of descriptions? Where are "You" hiding? In between the brain cells? Inside of your heart? Maybe in your thoughts? Who possesses the personality?

We know it's not the body, as the body is just a combination of cells that work the same in everybody. These cells multiply and divide, creating a different version of the body many times over the course of the body's life. So, beyond the body, where does "I" reside? Spend some time thinking about it; peel the layers of physical characteristics back.

We just determined above that the space we exist in and the particles we are comprised of are all one. So, where does the conflict between two egos exist? Logically, it is not between our physical selves. Our physical bodies carry on by themselves. No one is "in charge" or directs the body to divide billions of cells every second, to breathe, to digest food, to cleanse itself on the inside, etc. The body simply lives its own life, unaware of any owner or "I" who possesses it.

Is "I" a Personality?

To continue our search for ourselves, now that we've determined we are not the body, let's dissect the concept of a personality. Taking the physical characteristics out of the definition of "I," let's see how the separate personality is created.

A baby is born into this world. The pure awareness is manifested into a body that perceives worldly phenomena. There is no language, no labels, no separateness. But the body is born into a certain environment—parents, lifestyle, family members, socio-economic variables, etc. As the body grows, the environment shapes a program we call "personality" inside of the pure awareness born as a baby. A baby is told it has a name, that there are subjects and objects, good and evil, that it should do certain things and abstain from doing others, that it should believe in a certain religion, etc. That is how personality is shaped. We grow up with a certain automatic set of beliefs, concepts, and ideas, and as the environment around us changes (e.g., we move away to college, we meet a life partner, etc.), our personality changes accordingly.

What we call "personality" is nothing more than five ongoing processes: thinking, speaking, sensing, feeling emotions, and the bodily movements triggered by them. These processes are not the subject of experience; they are its content. They are what appears. The conclusion is unavoidable: it is not the person who is aware; the person is what is being perceived.

So, are "You" this personality? Is your true self a set of programs that you didn't choose to be born into? We will discuss the concept of choice in the next chapter, but beyond choosing your environment, can you truly say, "I am my personality"? Or to put it into a possessive form, which demonstrates the concept of the "I-doer" even better, who "owns" this personality? We've established that it's not the body, as the body is just a combination of biological characteristics common to all human beings and, on a deeper level, is just a vibration of quantum particles stemming from one unified field/space/void, so who is the "I" that the personality belongs to?

By now, we have established that "I" isn't a body or any of its organs or characteristics, including thoughts and feelings. It is also not personality, as that is just a combination of automated patterns of thinking and reactions, shaped by the environment the body exists in. Let's take it a step further and try to find where "we" exist in the dream space.

Where is "I" in the Dream Space?

To demonstrate further, take, for example, a nighttime dream. You see yourself inside the dream, but you don't know you are dreaming. For you, everything feels absolutely real—you speak, you think, you act, you feel. There are many other characters around you, each seemingly independent. They also talk, think, and make choices that surprise you. It's impossible to predict how any of them will act next. You can't read their minds. They all appear to be separate, independent beings.

But in truth, all of them are entirely and completely woven out of the very space of the dream itself. On their own, they can neither speak nor think—though it looks as if they can. They have no ability to be conscious. They are being conscious of!

And most importantly, not only they, but also the one you take yourself to be inside the dream (the main character in your dream) is, likewise, being conscious of.

When the dream ends, everything that seemed so real disappears like smoke from a fire. You just awoke from the "you" inside of your dream! Was there a separate "I" that your waking "I" was conscious of, in the dream space? Again, where is that separate "I" that the dream belonged to? It's definitely not the body, as your body was sleeping, and you could have had a totally different personality in the dream!

I hope by now you are beginning to understand the point: "I" does not exist as a separate independent entity. The universal aware space/void, which is God, as we determined earlier, is the only perceiver.

So now, when you awaken from a nighttime dream in that same aware space (in you), another kind of dream appears, what we call "the waking state." But in essence, it is the same kind of dream, where everything and everyone around "you" is woven of the same space but appears to be separate and independent of one another. All perceived phenomena, at their deep, sub-quantum level, consist of the same aware emptiness—of you. And just as in the nighttime dream, these phenomena have no author. There is no one who possesses free will or choice (we will explore the concept of the "Doer" of the "Ego" in the next section) or no one who "possesses" a personality or a body.

There are countless dream characters, but it is not they who awaken. It is the one and same aware space that awakens—the consciousness that has manifested itself as a multitude of seemingly independent tunnels of reality.

Within you, the character you once believed yourself to be continues to "awaken" other dream-like beings. Yet you, as the space of awareness in which this whole absurd play unfolds, remain untouched by it all. And at the very same time, everything that is perceived is woven out of you and is your continuous manifestation.

The way my Teacher Pasha would put it—both the dream state and the waking state are hallucinations of the same consciousness. The perceiver creates a reality out of itself, gets lost in it, identifies itself with the "main" character, and completely forgets that it is, itself, the fabric of the entire hallucination! It's akin to the body getting tangled in its own hair and mistakenly identifying itself with one of the hairs—now, that hair can have a conflict with "other" hairs or with the nose or with the left arm, as it forgets that it is the body, one uniform cohesive and undivided mechanism.

Now that we have logically arrived at the conclusion that everything perceived is woven out of you and is your continuous manifestation, to truly confirm and experience the realization that an independent "I" does not exist, and all there is is just one pure awareness, I offer you a practice of neti neti.

Neti neti is a classical method of self-inquiry in the Indian philosophical and spiritual tradition, primarily Advaita Vedānta, but also referenced in certain Upanishadic teachings and later yogic texts. The phrase literally means "not this, not that" and is used as a systematic approach to discern the true Self by negating everything that is not the Self.

In our lives, we are used to the concepts of subjects and objects, so neti neti offers you a chance to find, in your personal experience, the true "subject" or self that experiences the objects—the "I" we have been searching for in this chapter. As the premise for this practice, we understand that everything that is the object experienced as phenomena that come and go and are changing is not the subject that experiences.

Start by sitting somewhere comfortably, in silence, with no distractions. Close your eyes and calm your thoughts with as many deep breaths as you need.

Now, go through everything within your awareness to determine if it's the experience or the experiencer. Start with the body. The body is perceived and changes; therefore, neti.

Now, sensations—they also come and go, in and out of your awareness; thus, neti.

Next, thoughts—they arise and dissolve; neti.

Emotions—they fluctuate, last, and go away; again, neti.

Roles, identities, memories—all impermanent, constantly changing in your experience; neti.

Even subtle states (sleep, bliss, insight) are also observed and change; so, also neti.

When you put all neti aside after examining them, you will find the space in which all awareness appears, but even that space is perceived. Eventually, you will see that what remains is the silent, formless awareness in which all experiences appear and disappear. And that silent awareness is you. Neti neti peels back the layers of what exists in your experience and arrives at the root, where you cannot look behind the eye to "see the seer" and that eye, that awareness is all there is, and that is your true self.

I suggest you spend at least one quiet evening practicing neti neti before moving on to the next chapter.

Non-duality of All Being

> "Duality is the dream the mind weaves upon the screen of the Self.
> When the weaver is seen to be woven, and the screen seen to be the seer,
> the two dissolve into the One that never moved."
>
> - *Bṛhadāraṇyaka Upaniṣad 4.5.15*

Now that we found ourselves as the ultimate awareness and have hopefully set the objects in our experiences aside as not being us, let's dissect and destroy the concept of duality. Going back to the practice of neti neti, when we realize that our true self is the constant and unchanging witnessing awareness, we can also see that the objects perceived are non-dual to the subject itself. The perception does not exist without the perceiver.

Advaita Vedānta literally means "not two." The content of the awareness is non-dual of the awareness itself. The perceiver and the perception are fundamentally non-dual because both arise within the same unbroken field of awareness or the conscious aware space/void that we explored in Concept 1, above. What appears as a subject looking out upon an external world is, upon inquiry, revealed to be a conceptual division created by the mind.

A great example comes from *The Matrix,* a movie I love and that contains so much non-dual wisdom.

Neo is sitting with a group of children inside the Oracle's apartment. One boy is bending a spoon with his mind. Neo watches, confused.

The boy looks at him and says, "Do not try to bend the spoon. That's impossible. Instead... only try to realize the truth."

Neo asks, "What truth?"

The boy replies, "There *is* no spoon."

Neo looks at the spoon again.

The boy continues, "Then you'll see, it is not the spoon that bends... It is only yourself."

Think about it: if all thinking appears in this indivisible space/void, how can the perceived subject be separate from the object if everything is woven out of the same aware space? The perceiver—what we call the "I" that knows—is itself just another appearance in consciousness, no more inherent or independent than the objects it seems to perceive.

When this split is examined through practices like neti neti and direct self-inquiry, it becomes clear there is only the witnessing awareness in which both "observer" and "observed" arise and dissolve. In this recognition, perception is no longer experienced as a relationship between two separate entities, but as the Self knowing itself in various forms.

Going back to our example of the dream state, when you fall asleep, you, as the aware consciousness, start perceiving a story line of some characters who all appear to be separate from and act independently of one another. But when you awaken, you realize that all of those seemingly separate characters existed in the space of your dreaming consciousness. The same applies in the awakened state, where the consciousness perceives the same characters, just in a different state, which we call the awakened state.

But is consciousness of space where the dream characters appear different from the consciousness of space where awakened characters appear? No. As we determined earlier, as everything appears in one void/space that is conscious and where all phenomena arise and are made out of the same particles of this aware space.

To use another analogy, think of the Self/God/Awareness as a giant universal screen. The screen exists unaffected by the movie that plays on it. Movie characters run across the screen; they live, they love, they suffer, they die. The weather also changes—it rains, it hails, it snows; times of the day change, too, but the screen is unaffected by all of this. It just exists as the space where all of this appears. Yet, at the same time, you cannot take the movie off the screen and have it exist separately from it. It needs the screen to play out; it exists because of the screen. Yet the screen and the movie are one and the same—not two, not dualistic.

The same can be said about a mirror. A mirror is not dualistic to the reflection, as the reflection exists because of the mirror. The reflection cannot be taken out of the mirror and exist independent of it. The problem of the dualistic mind (or ego) is that, somehow, it finds itself as one of the characters in the movie on the screen or one of the parts of the reflection in the mirror, then associates itself with that separate character, and forgets itself as the screen or the mirror. This is where all suffering finds its roots.

When the screen finds itself as the screen, it does not mean the character ceases to exist; it just means the screen realizes that the character is not separate from the screen, but is just as temporary as all other phenomena appearing on the screen in the movie of Life.

This realization of the non-existence of the "I" is the literal death of all past experiences, life stories, relationships, and other dualistic aspects of one's life. That's what the title of my book describes: the process of the realization of the death of the imaginary ego and the realization that the true Self has always existed and will forever exist. The self-identification of oneself with the ego "I" (body, personality, thoughts—everything we discussed above) is nothing more than an illusion, and when the light of awareness and self-searching is shined on all those aspects in search of the "I," nothing can be found.

When I (I now only use this pronoun because the language of a narrative requires it to be used) first came across this realization through the process of neti neti, my life ended and restarted in a completely different light, as the self-identification completely shifted. The process of this realization took time for me, and it varies from person to person and based on the strength of the self-identification with their ego.

Mine was quite strong and took a lot of effort and concentration on a daily basis to gradually erode every false layer of identity, until the ego—the sense of being a separate, limited "I"—was revealed as unfindable. As each aspect of experience is examined and negated as "not me," I discovered that the ego has no independent existence; it is merely a bundle of thoughts, memories, and identifications arising within consciousness.

When the mind looks for this "I" that claims ownership of perception, action, fear, and desire, it finds nothing substantial, only a shifting pattern of appearances. This recognition is often described as the "death" of the ego, not because something real dies, but because the illusion of separateness loses its credibility. The illusionary self cannot die, as it never existed in the first place. What remains after this dissolution is the unconditioned awareness that was always present but overlooked: the Self, Brahman, the pure witnessing consciousness that is unborn, undivided, and untouched by the fluctuations of the mind. It's like releasing the spasm that was concentrating attention in one spot.

From the standpoint of Advaita Vedānta, this discovery is self-realization, for the seeker recognizes that the true Self is not an entity within the world but the very ground of all experience. The end of suffering follows naturally, not as an achievement but as the collapse of the mistaken identity that suffering depended on. Pain, pleasure, gain, loss, fear, and desire all belong to the imagined separate self; when that self is seen as illusory, these experiences lose their psychological grip.

The world continues to appear—as waves continue to ripple on the ocean— but the realized one knows themselves as the water, not the wave. Suffering ends because the root of suffering, the belief in a finite "me" struggling within an external world, is seen to have never truly existed. In this clarity, what remains is effortless peace, a freedom that is not attained but uncovered, and the understanding that the Self was always whole, free, and complete.

It is important to understand, I do not mean your illusory world ends; no, it continues existing, and there could still be "suffering" or negative experiences for the character, but those experiences do not belong to anyone and thus lose their grip, self-liberate, and dissolve. When consciousness stops getting lost in the myriad thoughts about suffering that belong to the independent "I," the spams release, and all experiences simply come and go, without being chronicled as stories of one's life.

To my reader, I want to say that this realization is the ultimate, most magnificent culmination of any human life. If one is blessed with the ability to discover this truth, the universe becomes one's playground, and life becomes abundantly delicious and fulfilling. This state of awareness cannot really be described in words, but the best attempt at describing it would be to imagine if you finally found your home—you have arrived after decades of searching. And now, there is nowhere else to go, nothing to worry about, and nothing to fear—just pure pleasure of existing in the world that feels like home.

I do have to say that, as mentioned above, this realization cannot just come from reading the words or listening to your teacher. It comes through your own self-discovery. The words are just pointers telling you where to look, but the constant effort of ceasing to self-identify with temporary experiences and phenomena will take some time. For me, it took over a year. And even still, the ego attempts to sneak in and take over, because this is how our whole world is built.

Unless you become a monk and denounce worldly living altogether, we all still are social creatures in this māyā[3] and have to go on with our daily lives. Advaita Vedānta teaches that this māyā is the power of appearance

---

[3] Māyā in Sanskrit is the principle by which the one, indivisible reality appears as a world of separate forms, identities, and experiences.

that makes the one, non-dual Reality seem to become the manifold world of forms, names, and experiences. It is not an illusion in the sense of "nonexistence," nor a real entity in its own right. Instead, it is described as neither real nor unreal, a mysterious principle that cannot be fully defined but can be understood through its effects.

Māyā veils the true nature of Brahman (pure consciousness) and simultaneously projects the appearance of duality—much like clouds that hide the sun while also creating shifting patterns of light and shadow. My Teacher Pasha describes it as the hypnotizing, enchanting power that, by use of words and labels/concepts, always creates the appearance that there are, in fact, two.

The way our language is structured, with possessive pronouns. The way forms appear to our human vision as separate objects. The way words attach separate meanings to phenomena arising out of the same space. All of this is the sorcery of māyā, which we, as God, created for ourselves, and now just fail to recognize.

"Why?" you may ask. Why would an omnipotent God consciousness hypnotize itself and be stuck in an illusion?

The answer is in the question itself, but that, again, is just rhetoric.

If God is omnipotent, He can create a rock He cannot lift. But if He cannot lift a rock He created, how is He omnipotent? By the same analogy, if God created an illusion to experience/know Himself to the fullest through dual aspects of being, His creation is so craftily done that He Himself believed the illusion.

It is important, though, to stop asking these questions and getting lost in the rhetoric, as true answers don't exist, and there isn't any actual "meaning" or "purpose" to this.

It just is, and that's what you find through neti neti, that everything just is. By creating words, shaping them into concepts, and attempting to explain that "is-ness," the mind only gets further and further away from home, which is just empty, luminous space that is aware of itself.

Although some logical reasoning is required to get on the path of enlightenment and for it to make sense to a non-awakened mind, asking questions and getting lost in the rhetoric makes God-consciousness shift away from its empty, luminous nature into yet another tunnel of illusory reality. Following rhetoric and seeking answers will never end, as the mind will keep creating more distractions from God/true nature.

It is just as simple as remaining quietly aware. I remember my reaction of shock when Pasha told one of his students in a meeting to, "Just shut up." To the ego, it is an insult, but all it truly is is a loving direction to stop getting lost in thoughts, concepts, and words, and instead to remain silent and simply aware. That simple, quiet awareness is God—our true nature. Attachment to words and concepts is what carries God away into an illusory tunnel of reality.

Remember how, in the beginning of the book, I stated that, to truly attain self-realization, very intense focus is required, along with earnestness and self-discipline? This is where it is needed—in this process of building new self-identification, of denouncing the old and the temporary, of constant self-searching, and of not getting lost in the rhetoric, all of which can be quite challenging.

When you start practicing neti neti or other forms of meditation (some of which I will offer in this book), your mind will revolt; it will want to go back to the usual and habitual patterns. You will start noticing lack of energy, lethargy, apathy, and nihilistic tendencies; your mind will create more questions and reasons to stop the self-searching, to retract attention back to its usual focus. With constant self-searching, you may work your mind up so much, it hits a stupor, and all of this will stop making any sense.

If you give in to these tricks, you will never attain self-realization. The practice of negating the Neti must be constant and earnest. But it's not meant to torture you or become a burdensome chore. Simply give yourself time.

Take a break, breathe, sleep on it, and then come back to this chapter and your neti neti as much as you can. Be quiet, be still, observe, and come back to the practice when you can. With time, this realization will unfold inside of a pure, undisturbed mind that is unburdened by the concepts of duality.

Why Does Duality Appear in Oneness?

You may be wondering at this point, as I for sure did when I first learned about these concepts, "Why does duality take place? Why does non-dual pure awareness fool itself into seeing itself as only part of itself?"

There are different theories about this, all philosophical. In reality, nobody knows the true reason, as everything in this world just is. Is impossible for a human mind to fully grasp the magic of what the quantum field of awareness truly is, and, as I stated above, the mind can only explain through words and concepts, which do not exist in our true natural state. Asking this question is yet again getting caught up in never-ending rhetoric and shifting attention from your true nature. However, for the sake of our human intelligence coming to terms with this, let's explore the most logical theories for duality.

Advaita Vedānta teaches that duality appears within oneness only because of a fundamental misperception rooted in avidyā, or ignorance. In its true nature, reality is Brahman—one, indivisible, and without a second—yet the mind, which operates through categorization and contrast, overlays distinctions upon this seamless field of being. This process, known as adhyāsa or superimposition, is similar to mistaking a rope for a snake: nothing actually changes in the rope, yet a false appearance is taken as real. In the same way, the body-mind identifies itself as a separate perceiver, and everything else is then experienced as "other," giving rise to the subject-object split.

Through the power of māyā, the undivided Self appears fragmented, just as one sun seems to become many when reflected in rippling water. From the absolute standpoint, duality never truly arises; it exists only from the limited perspective of the mind. When ignorance is removed through inquiry and insight, it becomes clear that the one was never two and duality was merely an appearance projected upon the unchanging reality of pure consciousness.

The human mind is the root of separation; it is where it appears, although the human mind is the way for the absolute to know itself. Remember the paradox that the absolute can create an illusion so perfect, it gets fooled by it? This is exactly it—the human mind is a perfect way to experience the vast capabilities of the absolute, but it is also the limitation in which the absolute forgets its own original perfection and omnipotence.

For less sophisticated minds unable to grasp the non-dual superimposition concepts of Advaita Vedānta, we have similar religious tales in many dualistic religions. The Fallen Angel is a concept appearing in many world religions, where a holy being, who was once God's brother (truly, God in itself), falls from Heaven to find itself in a world of sin and temptation, and hides in the "underworld," afraid of God's fury and punishment. This is a simplistic tale of duality—an explanation of how the holy divides itself into the unholy and creates the opposition of good and evil. But even in these simplistic tales, the non-holy originally comes from the holy—everything appears in one Heaven, one original void.

The most rational explanation for duality, taking the complex Advaita concepts and the simplistic religious tales together, is that there simply could not be a non-dual reality that could know itself. How could the eye see itself? How could one know oneself without the other to reflect off? How could good exist without evil, love without hate, pleasure without pain?

Duality is at the core of self-realization, as there would be nothing to realize in the absence of the dual reality. From the point of this initial separation from one into many, it appears that God or consciousness lost itself in the dual world, akin to the Fallen Angel mentioned above, creating many paths back to itself.

Think about it: across the world's great religious traditions, a shared theme quietly emerges despite vast differences in doctrine and symbolism: the primary purpose of existence is to move from a state of separation, confusion, or suffering toward a deeper alignment with what is ultimately real, good, or sacred. In the Abrahamic traditions—Judaism, Christianity, and Islam—life is understood as a journey of remembering, loving, and aligning with God, cultivating ethical living, and returning to the divine presence.

Hinduism frames existence as an opportunity to realize the identity of the individual Self with Brahman, dissolving ignorance and attaining liberation. Buddhism presents life as a path of awakening, revealing the nature of suffering and freeing the mind from grasping and delusion. Taoism emphasizes harmony with the Tao, the natural flow of existence, inviting a life of balance, humility, and effortless action. Many Indigenous and animistic traditions view existence as a continual act of living in right relationship with the Earth, the community, the spirits, and the ancestors. Even humanistic or philosophical systems locate life's purpose in the cultivation of wisdom, virtue, meaning, and self-actualization.

Though the metaphysical frameworks differ, these traditions converge on a single insight: life is not random or meaningless, but a profound opportunity for inner growth, awakening, and the transcendence of the narrow self in favor of a richer, more unified experience of reality.

The plethora of these traditions, the multitude of paths, and the diversity of methods—to attain this true unity with God—are nothing but pointers to realizing that there never was anything but One God. It's a plethora of paths without a path, a multitude of travels without a traveler—as once you see that everything is and has always been one You, which is the origin of everything, all paths, travels, and concepts vanish.

As my dear Teacher Pasha says, all spiritual traditions are like ladders into the skies/Heaven. We climb those ladders through pain and suffering, but when we reach the top and look back, we realize that there was never a ladder or the one who climbed it. God, as the absolute reality, can be absolutely wrong about itself. But when the absolute reality is found, the illusion falls off, revealing the true and eternal space, which is God, which is self.

How is Duality Shaped in Humans?

With the understanding that duality is needed for the absolute to know itself, Advaita tells us that māyā (illusion of duality) appeared in Sat Chit Ananda (the original conscious void, or Existence-Consciousness-Bliss, if translated literally) as different phenomena, shapes, and beings. Among the different manifestations of māyā, humans are deemed to be the "crown of creation," i.e., beings in which the absolute consciousness can find its way back to itself. The Crown of Creation has the potential to be God in human form, where the world is one's playground, and any intentions or wishes are realized instantaneously through the absolute power of one's true nature.

Below is the demonstration of how the original energy (I use the Vedic Sat Chit Ananda as the name for that foundational void/space) manifests itself into human form, known as the Seven Bodies. The concept of the Seven Bodies comes across various religious and metaphysical traditions, all stating the same idea: that a human is manifested out of seven bodies that also have seven corresponding planes of existence.

The Pyramid of Manifestation, pictured below, begins at its widest and most expansive point with Sat Chit Ananda, the non-dual essence that underlies and permeates all existence. It is a single, seamless reality that is timeless, self-luminous, and inherently whole (as we discussed earlier). It is not a description of three separate qualities; it is an attempt to point toward the ineffable nature of the One that cannot be divided. In Advaita, recognizing oneself as Sat Chit Ananda is synonymous with liberation, for it reveals that the true Self was never finite, bound, or lacking, but always the infinite fullness of being itself.

From this infinite ground of being (this empty void/space that knows itself), the spectrum of human embodiment gradually narrows into seven distinct bodies, each representing a further condensation of the original unity. Out of this unity, the first to emerge is the Body of Awareness, the subtle field in which consciousness recognizes itself as the witness of all experience. This then refines into the Body of Presence, the quiet inner luminosity that suffuses perception with a sense of immediacy and beingness.

As the descent continues, the essence condenses into the Energetic Body, the dynamic layer through which life-force moves, patterns take shape, and intention begins to influence form. Beneath these subtle dimensions lie the three denser bodies: the Sensory Body, which translates vibration into perception; the Mental Body, which organizes thought, memory, and interpretation; and finally, the Physical Body, the most tangible and contracted/dense expression of the original non-dual source.

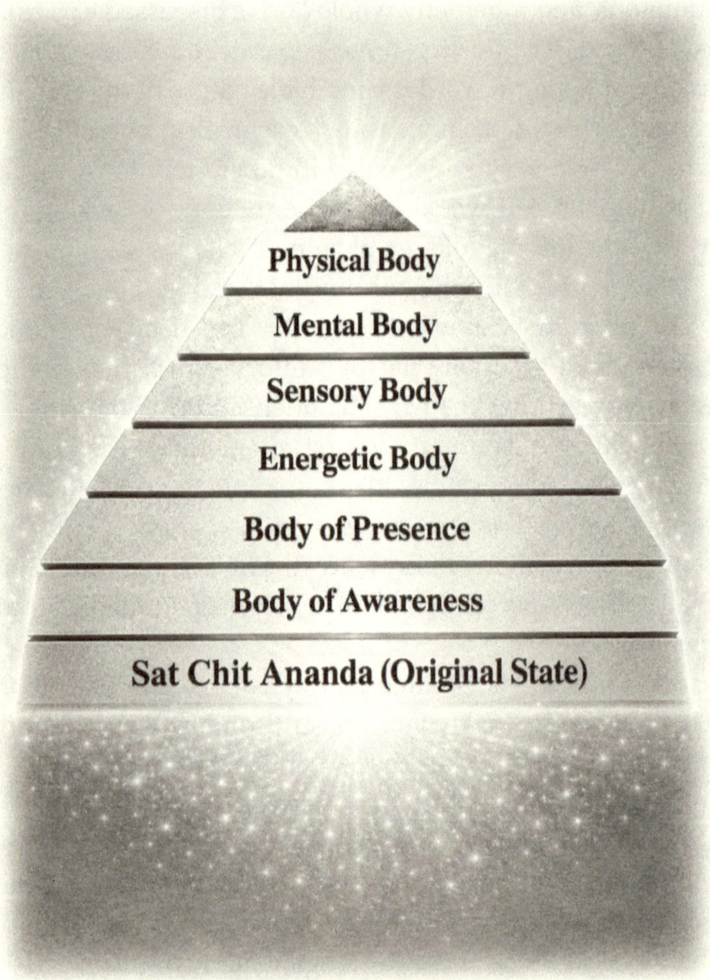

Within each of these seven bodies exist seven inner planes, and individuals with heightened or unusual capacities may learn to perceive or access these hidden domains, touching layers of reality that remain veiled to ordinary awareness.

For example, Reiki masters operate in the plane of Energy (the energetic body), whereas so-called psychics or foretellers have access to the Mental plane, which contains the Akashic records of all there ever was, is, or will be known to the mental bodies. The plane of Presence is where all masters of meditation and presence practice. The abilities to access these planes are sometimes mistaken for spiritual awakening or complete realization, when in fact they are still just manifestations of the dual reality.

Consciousness born into human form manifests itself very differently in every plane and body, depending on each individual form's environment, family, social variables, genetic characteristics, and so on. But each human is a dense form of the absolute, manifested through the seven bodies; each body is made of the same fundamental particles manifested out of the void/space.

Each human (mind) sees the world in a unique way and considers that way to be the only true one, but that is the nature of māyā or illusion—anything can appear and disappear in the absolute. And as long as the identification with the separate human exists in the consciousness born into a human body, those different "truths" will manifest themselves and confirm themselves in that human's subjective reality.

The absolute consciousness that shines its light of awareness through a mind that sees itself as limited manifests that which appears believable to the limited mind. All convictions, beliefs, and points of view are nothing but limited manifestations of the absolute consciousness. In reality, there are no truths or absolutes—everything just is. Everything appears in the absolute consciousness, lasts, and disappears. The only things that define the different-appearing phenomena are just labels of words that the human mind places on them. Take off the labels, and everything collapses into one field playing with its own energies. Beautiful, isn't it?

And liberating! No more searching for the ultimate truth, no more arguing about who's right and wrong, no more seeking for the "correct" religion. They all just are; take them as they are, let them last, and let them go.

When one believes in aliens, another in angels, and a third in elves and mermaids, they all are simply affirming their beliefs through the manifestations the universal consciousness experiences in them. All are real and not real at the same time. All just are as they are, just as everything else just is. Beautiful play of energies in an absolute potential of our unified consciousness.

Here, it is very important to understand that the Pyramid of Manifestation of the absolute into the relative shapes can only be explained and conceptualized with words to a certain extent. It is as close as it can be to make sense to our human mind. But in true absolute reality, as I already stated before, the words that form concepts do not exist, so describing the absolute in relative human words is like trying to fit a square peg into a round hole (or, as we say in Russian, "fit a globe inside of an owl"), i.e., force a description onto something that cannot be described.

Sat Chit Ananda, or our absolute non-dual state, is akin to dreamless sleep. We all experience it, so this analogy will make sense to everybody. In dreamless sleep, no concepts exist, including words, thoughts, characters, shapes, or objects, etc. Even the body or the "main character" does not exist or isn't being aware of. There are literally "not two." It's just the absolute nothing that is aware of itself.

Can we operate with words in dreamless sleep? No. Are there "others" or even "me"? No. Are there boundaries, time, and limitations? No again.

That's what our true nature feels like, so you can see that the manifestation into our relative reality is necessary for the absolute to know its full potential to manifest into anything, but that anything is not absolute, as nothing can be labeled "absolute" when broken down to its source.

Spend some time with this, as I know this is hard to grasp. I would go back to neti neti to fully live this in your experience and to feel this aware nothingness when you peel all of the layers of "not this" down to the foundational source.

Chapter 4

Concept 2 of the Teaching: The Doer/Chooser/Actor

"The ego builds its palace out of dust,
calls it 'I,' and kneels before its own illusion.
Break the palace, and you will see—
only the sky was ever real."
~Omar Khayyam

THE DISCUSSION OF non-duality and the true nature of ourselves always ends with one asking the same question: "What about free choice? Aren't we in charge of our lives and can choose a path, be it a spiritual one or otherwise?"

The answer is that there is no free choice or any choice at all, and this answer is the ultimate stumbling block that many fail to overcome on the way to liberation and self-realization. The idea of a doer/chooser/actor/maker is so inherent in the way our society operates that breaking it requires not only earnestness and focus, but also the ability to completely release all control, give in, give up, and cease existing. Tough ask, isn't it?

Let's break it down, like we did with our journey of dissecting the reality to see that all is one. In Sanskrit, the term ahamkara literally means "I-maker" or "ego-constructor." Ahamkara in Advaita is an illusion, a nonexistent parasite that feeds off the absolute energy and limits manifestation. It is the function of the mind that creates the sense of being a separate individual who perceives, chooses, acts, and owns experiences.

Let's go back to our Seven Bodies diagram/Pyramid of Manifestation. In that model, ahamkara—the ego-constructing function of the mind—serves as the hinge upon which the entire illusion of duality turns. It arises within the Mental Body as the subtle impulse that claims ownership over thoughts, actions, and experiences, giving consciousness the false impression of being a separate entity navigating the world. Once ahamkara takes root, the denser layers of embodiment—the Sensory Body and Physical Body—are interpreted as "me," while the subtler layers are perceived as "mine," reinforcing the subject-object split that defines duality.

How does this appear in the Mental Body? Let's think back to our childhood... Before you knew that your name was "Bobby" or "Anastasia," did you consider yourself as a separate being, making choices independent of other bodies called "Mom" or "Dad"? You may not remember this, but you did not, and science proves that the "I-others" distinction does not exist until age three.

If you have young children, you can see it in them. The concept of separateness only comes with language. To a child, the words "I" and "You" are just words, and they may use them interchangeably when telling stories. When you first name a child, they don't associate the word with themselves—they only learn to do that through repeated patterns of recognizing that, when that word is said, it usually applies to them.

The child is growing, learning, playing, and socializing, and in each of those facets of his/her development, adults tell him/her what's good or bad, and how he/she should act.

I hear, "You ate all of your cereal. Good girl, Anastasia!" Now I know that finishing the food is good.

But when I hear, "You made a mess on the table. Bad girl, Anastasia," I know that messes are bad.

Now I am being told I can choose to be bad or good—to eat or to make a mess. But before I was taught that, was there an "I" making those choices? If so, where did it exist? In my brain? In my body? In between the letters A-n-a-s-t-a-s-i-a? Remember our discussion of Mary and John—where exactly in the body does the chooser reside?

In fact, ahamkara has no independent existence; it is only a pattern of identification arising within awareness. It appears someone is making a choice, but in reality, energy just travels based on its usual patterns. "We" are nothing but energies programmed by our environments to act a certain way. To act without an "actor"—the act is automatic. Let's dissect this, if you are still not convinced.

A choice is an act, meaning our body acts based on a choice of some sort. For example, you have a choice to drink tea or coffee. Two thoughts arise in your brain: 1) tea? 2) coffee? When those thoughts appear, the body, based on its preset programs, reacts a certain way (e.g., "coffee gives me anxiety" versus "tea calms me down"). Based on those automatic predispositions, you choose tea. It appears as a choice you made, but in reality, it's nothing but a combination of preset programs you have been acquiring during the course of your life.

To dissect this scientifically, every movement/choice of the body is determined by electrical impulses in the brain, generated by billions of dividing cells. Eighty-six billion neurons fire in complex patterns, each producing up to ten impulses per second. Where, between these eighty-six billion impulses, is the chooser? Who directs the impulses?

Every thought, feeling, or inclination toward a thought is simply witnessed at the moment it arises; just a split second earlier, and the awareness knew nothing of it and had no technical access to its emergence. Yet, these thoughts and feelings drive the body's actions.

Without the appearance of the thought or sensation of hunger, the body would not move at all; without the spontaneous arising of "tea or coffee?" or "left or right?" no choice would ever be made. Decisions unfold by themselves, and their outcome is unknowable until it appears. This is how life proceeds, moment by moment. We have no technical access to choose our thoughts—how could we, if they get determined by eighty-six billion impulses in the brain? Is there a "menu" of thoughts we can view before a certain thought ("tea or coffee?") appears?

To truly grasp this, I offer you this practice: try cultivating presence at the very boundary where thoughts first arise—the thin, luminous edge between pure awareness and the first stirrings of mental activity. This practice begins by resting in a quiet, alert stillness, allowing the mind to settle without trying to suppress anything.

Take a few deep breaths, and try to calm your mind as much as you can, but without effort. The practice should be peaceful and not forceful.

At first, you will start noticing thoughts as they appear. Try to just notice them, without following any one thought into more thoughts on the same subject. Just notice.

As attention becomes more refined, you begin to sense thoughts not when they are fully formed, but at the very moment they start to emerge, like the first ripple on an otherwise calm surface. Instead of following the thought or giving it a name, you stay with the subtle impulse before it becomes a narrative—an energetic twitch, a faint vibration, a pre-thought pressure.

At this boundary, ask yourself: do you know what the next thought will be? Is there a menu of thoughts you can choose from? You will see very clearly that there isn't one and that you don't know the next thought until after it arises. You witness it in the moment of its appearance.

This is the birthplace of ahamkara, the point where awareness contracts into "I am thinking," even though there is no "I" who is thinking. Thoughts simply arise, and you witness them as pure awareness.

By remaining present at this boundary, you begin to see that the ego does not generate thoughts; it claims them after they arise. You do not choose thoughts; they simply come. The sense of "I" arrives a fraction of a second after the thought appears, attaching ownership to something that was already unfolding on its own. In this micro-space, before identification, before naming, before grasping, you witness thoughts as spontaneous movements of the field, not as personal creations.

Over time, this reveals that ahamkara is not an entity but a habit of appropriation, a reflexive gesture of claiming ownership over impersonal mental activity. When that habit becomes visible, it begins to dissolve, and a thought loses its power to define or confine the Self. What remains is presence itself: a spacious, unclaimed awareness in which thoughts arise and vanish like sparks in open sky, leaving the clarity of the true Self unobscured.

If you try to go into an ashram (a temple of a non-dual tradition like Advaita) to seek this knowledge, the master in the ashram gives the student a simple task: "If you are the author of your thoughts, sit still for one full day and do not think. At all. Not a single letter or word."

Thoughts about the absence of thoughts also count as thoughts. The student tries hard not to think any thoughts, but they keep flooding in without any control or power to stop them.

When the student inevitably fails, the master gives the next assignment: "Think only one delightful thought for the entire day." If one could do that, one would be happy for life—but of course, this, too, ends in failure.

The conclusion is unavoidable: free will, personal choice, and conscious control do not exist. Any question or thought that appears to arise "from consciousness" does not belong to it; all of it simply appears within awareness, unbidden and uncontrollable.

Bringing this to modern science yet again, physics and neuroscience increasingly suggest that what we experience as "choice" is already set in motion before conscious awareness ever claims it, echoing insights long held in the ashrams of non-dual traditions. Experiments in quantum neurobiology and delayed-choice phenomena show that, at the most fundamental level, events unfold probabilistically within a unified field before the mind constructs the narrative of a personal decision. So, the ego "reality" is nothing but a delayed interpretation of the automatic processes occurring within consciousness.

One of the most intriguing experiments often discussed in quantum neurobiology comes from the work of Dr. Anirban Bandyopadhyay and his team, who studied the tiny structures inside neurons called microtubules, which play a role in shaping of cells. In 2014, using an ultra-sensitive scanning device, Bandyopadhyay's group observed high-frequency vibrational patterns within microtubules that behaved in ways classical physics couldn't fully explain. These vibrations appeared to switch states in a coordinated, almost rhythmic manner, hinting at a kind of internal quantum coherence on their own.

The reason why this matters in the question of choice is that these micro-vibrations happened before any electrical signal traveled through the neuron—suggesting that at least part of what drives neural activity originates in a domain more subtle than the level of ordinary electrochemical signaling. In simple terms: the body seems to begin "stirring" toward a movement or decision in a place far below where the conscious mind ever becomes involved.

These studies prove that our decisions begin forming in the quiet quantum depths of the nervous system long before the ego arrives to claim, "I chose that." So again, the biological structure that we call *ourselves*, a.k.a. the human body, moves and acts according to these deep quantum reactions that occur spontaneously, depending on the environment programmed into them, without any independent being who "owns" the body choosing its movements or acts.

In addition, studies like the Libet readiness potential (RP) demonstrate that the brain initiates an action several hundred milliseconds before a person becomes conscious of having "chosen" it. Dr. Benjamin Libet set out to measure exactly when a person becomes aware of making a decision. Participants were asked to perform a simple action, such as flexing a finger, whenever they felt the spontaneous urge to do so, while their brain activity was monitored.

Libet found something astonishing: the brain showed a clear buildup of electrical activity, known as the readiness potential, several hundred milliseconds before the participant consciously felt they had "decided" to move. In other words, the body had already begun preparing the action, quietly and automatically, before the mind stepped in to claim authorship.

Libet himself described consciousness not as the initiator of the act but more like a latecomer who notices what is already unfolding. This experiment, simple as it was, opened a profound doorway: if the impulse to act begins before awareness knows it, then the ego cannot be the true originator of choice. It merely arrives afterward and takes credit for a process already underway—a finding that mirrors the contemplative Advaita insight that ahamkara claims ownership over movements that never belonged to it in the first place.

When viewed together, these findings reveal a striking pattern: the impulse toward action arises silently in the deep layers of the system, within electrical, quantum, and neural fluctuations, long before the ego steps in to say, "I decided." Conscious choice is thus not the origin but the echo of an underlying process already in motion. What appears as free will is the delayed recognition of an event that has already emerged from the field.

In this way, modern physics and neuroscience illuminate what the ancient non-dual traditions described: the ego does not choose; it only arrives a moment too late, taking credit for the spontaneous unfolding of the universe within itself. The ego is, in reality, a mental construct of one's mind that seeks to exist through possessing. At the fundamental level, however, the ego does not exist.

To me, the analogy that makes the most sense is one where we liken our individual "selves" (bodies that think, talk, and act) to an Alexa/Echo speaker or a Google voice speaker. Each individual Alexa is loaded with software to understand voice and language. Each Alexa learns the preferences of its owner and automatically suggests playlists, recipes, timers, etc., based on a pattern of previous actions. Does each Alexa have an independent ego? Is there an individual being behind Alexa who chooses and possesses its actions? Of course not. But Alexa (except for its physical shape) is just like a human—it is a physical container that listens, talks, and acts depending on the content of what is loaded into its operational system.

We are all Alexas on the foundational level, but the mental construct of ahamkara hypnotizes us into believing we somehow control what's loaded into our operational system and decide how to treat such content.

Spend some time with this. Not just the knowledge, but the practice offered above. Realize, in your own practical experience, by shining the earnest light of awareness into the boundary of thoughts' appearance, that thoughts are spontaneous, and so are the feelings and decisions that they trigger.

This earnest practice, if performed with complete dedication and honesty, destroys the concept of the "I-doer" once and for all, freeing the pure God consciousness of what we truly are into uninhibited beautiful existence, outside of any limitations, concepts, or "others." This death of the "I" is the actual start of your true life, which never began and will never end.

Understanding How the "I" Continues to Exist

Most people who achieve the realization of the non-existence of the "I/ego" live outside of the regular modern world—they go to temples or ashrams, become monks, and spend their lives meditating and living in non-duality. For me and most people who have children and other worldly ties, such path is not an option. This is why many will fail in true and complete self-realization, as our world is built by the ego, survives and functions through the ego, and divides and conquers for the ego.

It is thus essential for those of us who cannot denounce the worldly living to notice and understand how the ego thrives in our usual social environments and to unhook ourselves from those usual environmental patterns.

"I" in a child

The imagined "I" is not born from freedom or spontaneity. It arises as an idea in consciousness, shaped by inherited social and familial programs. As my examples in the previous chapter demonstrate, a child is shaped to believe that he/she is the doer/chooser/responsible party. Mother's praise, Father's criticism, the endless pattern of carrot and stick: "Anastasia, you failed," "Bobby, you're a good boy," "Don't get your shirt dirty," "Be responsible," "Make proper choices."

For a child, this fictional self is then launched into games, fantasies, and dream worlds, where it tries on roles—sea creature, Rapunzel, Spider-Man—switching identities as easily as changing costumes. For a child, those identities are just as real as the "Bobby" who is a good or bad boy, depending on the day.

However, at some point, consciousness becomes so engrossed in the game, it begins to believe it is the character it is playing. (Remember our discussion, that the absolute can create an illusion so believable, it itself believes it.) Self-identification occurs. This usually happens by age seven.

The first illusion emerges: "I control. I choose," because of our parents' constantly telling us we do. Society amplifies the fantasy, insisting that certain feelings are unacceptable, certain thoughts should not be spoken, and certain emotions should be suppressed. And although these impulses arise automatically at the physical and mental levels, the imaginary character is burdened with the imagined responsibility for them, imposed by the social upbringing. Fiction becomes a functional entity—a supposed thinker, decider, regulator, and gatekeeper of emotions and behavior.

But this "I" soon encounters alternatives: sometimes its choices fail; sometimes they seem to succeed; and in the rare coincidence when an imagined intention aligns with an external event, the ego crowns itself victorious, like believing that a fruit fell because a crow landed on a branch, even though it was ripe and would have fallen anyway.

To put it simply, there is always one version of events in the present moment—the circumstances will align in a way that will make one scenario unfold (e.g., a child, threatened by a bully, runs away and leaves his friend behind to be beaten up), but the ego has many versions (if "I" was brave enough back then, I could have stayed and beaten up the bully and become the most popular kid in school). Shame and guilt quickly follow. Family, society, and the entire ancestral line constantly point out how the ego has "failed," cultivating a deep sense of personal wrongness.

Or, with the same example, if the circumstances unfolded in a way where a child did not run away and had actually saved his friend from the bully, then the ego would have crowned itself as a "hero" for making a choice to be brave, and the social recognition would follow. But the ego variants rarely coincide with the actual, singular way reality unfolds in any given moment, and this lack of coinciding produces guilt, shame, fear, and blame.

"I" Opposite "Others"

Then comes judgment of others: because they, too, allegedly have free choice, so they could have behaved better or been kinder and more attentive, if "they" had been put in the same circumstances; thus, the victim-perpetrator dynamic arises. Now, we have "others" the ego can blame for the reality not going the way it wants.

If "I" fail, surely someone else is to blame: e.g., the wrong school, the wrong environment, the wrong parents. Concepts like childhood trauma and lack of love and attention begin to flourish to shift the blame from the "I" to "others." In imagination, the ego punishes those it perceives as responsible. The world divides into "us" and "them."

The ego then seeks self-confirmation through others: how they color it, evaluate it, reflect on it. The entire practice of psychology/therapy reinforces this: "you" dig deeper, finding the "others" responsible for your failures. Through psychology, the ego thrives and self-confirms even more, leading the pure awareness of God further and further away from its true, beautiful, nondualist nature.

Ultimately, this creates the figure of the sufferer—the controller who desperately wants approval yet fails constantly, blames itself, judges others, and lives in perpetual inner tension. "I don't want to suffer" becomes another lie, because suffering provides the ego with its only sense of existence. Pain becomes its investment, its nourishment, the evidence that "I am real."

It then attempts to switch roles, to become the aggressor instead of the victim, but others are caught in the same illusion and resist becoming victims themselves—so the ego is struck back even harder, reinforcing its suffering. Have you noticed how, even though we all say we want to end suffering, we carry "our" pain with almost a sense of pride or achievement? We contrast our pain to that of the others to reinforce how much stronger and more resilient we are. We savor and relish every detail when we tell the stories of our suffering to others; we cling to "our" pain as a means of separating ourselves from others.

Over time, the division between inner and outer collapses. Initially, the threats seem to come from outside, but since the ego cannot resolve them externally, it drags them inward and punishes them in its imagination. An entire cast of characters accumulates within: what began as a small drama circle becomes a full drama theater. By fifty years old, a person may still be arguing with a boy from kindergarten who wiped a booger on them or said something rude.

Inside, the mind becomes both the patient and the psychiatrist in its own asylum. Or the judge, the prosecutor, the defender, and the defendant in its own internal court. When dogs bark outside, on the street, one can run away; but when they bark inside your own head, escape becomes impossible. The inner space becomes so unbearable, like a mental coma, that the ego flees outward into creativity, work, spiritual pursuits, parenting, and especially relationships with "others."

"I" in relationships

In relationships, two waves of the same ocean mistakenly perceive themselves as separate both from the ocean and from each other. These imagined selves try to hold each other, worship, desire, avoid, manipulate, judge, and cling, never realizing they are not two forces trying to grasp each other, but one essence pretending to be divided.

When egos enter into relationships, polarizing conflict and drama are inevitable, and modern society demonstrates just that: we are living in an era when the global divorce rate is four out of ten, with some countries being six or even eight out of ten. We call it "feminism," "personal values," or "self-love," but in reality, it's all nothing but the drama theater that the ego puts on to reinforce its own existence opposite the "others." In true nondual reality, relationships do not exist; they are just a play of the energy of one source, not separate from each other.

"I" in time

And then, of course, there is the concept of linear time. Time feeds the ego and duality by creating the past, present, and future; "my experiences" and "my memories." In the unified field of consciousness, there is no time, but for the individual "I," time suddenly appears—because that "I" is constantly failing in its own story.

What we call "my thoughts" are nothing more than echoes of this past. Every drive, desire, worry, ambition—

an entire virtual graveyard, claimed by a phantom that does not truly exist. The past is gone, the future has not yet arrived, and whatever we call the future instantly becomes the past the moment it appears. Where, then, is the *present* between them?

In reality, time itself does not exist. What we call "time" is nothing more than the mind's attempt to organize its own discomfort. The past exists only as memory traces—stories the ego revisits to justify its sense of identity. While the future is merely a projection designed to escape the pain of confronting the present moment. In Advaita Vedānta, time is understood as one of the great superimpositions of māyā, a great illusion; a cognitive lens through which the non-dual Self appears fragmented into a before and after.

Consciousness/space/void itself never moves; only thoughts about movement arise within it. The individual "I," unable to bear its own imagined inadequacy, constructs a timeline filled with regrets behind it and hopes or fears ahead, mistaking these mental flickers for objective reality. But the present is not a point wedged between past and future. It is the timeless field in which both arise and dissolve.

Past and future have no independent existence outside the thought that recalls or anticipates them. In direct awareness, when attention is no longer fixated on the stories of "me," time collapses back into the stillness from which it emerged. What remains is the changeless presence of consciousness, untouched by the events it seems to witness. From this standpoint, time is not a backdrop against which life unfolds; it is a mental mirage, appearing and disappearing within the one Reality that is eternally now.

Think about it. Can you ever experience or grasp the past or the future? Again, if you are earnest and remain still, you realize everything already "is" now in the present moment, even the memories of the past are now. And the term "moment" is not really a moment that is separate from the previous moment—it is just the ongoing now.

Can you tell when the previous moment ended and this one began? Can you see or perceive the boundaries?

Of course not. Because the reality of time is woven into the void/space we discussed in Chapter 1. It just is. It never appeared, will never disappear, and has no boundaries, beginning, or end. Remember the example of the dreamless sleep? Does time exist there? No. Just like other concepts of linear minds, it does not.

Here's an old folk story to help you understand this better:

A man once decided to chase "tomorrow." He woke up early and said, "Today, I'm going to reach it."

He walked forward. After a while, he stopped and asked himself, "Am I in tomorrow yet?"

"No... This is still today." So, he kept walking.

Hours passed. Miles passed.

"Now?" he asked. Still—today.

Frustrated, he ran. "If I move fast enough," he thought, "I'll catch it." He ran until he was exhausted.

Collapsed on the ground, he whispered, "How far away is tomorrow?"

An old woman passing by laughed softly and said, "You can walk for a thousand miles, and you will never step into tomorrow."

He looked at her, confused. "Why not?"

"Because, whenever you arrive," she said, "it's always today."

Let's go back to our example of a screen with a movie playing on it, to understand this even better. The story seems to unfold in time—scene after scene, past leading into future. You remember what just happened, and you anticipate what comes next. It feels continuous. But all of that—the memory of the last scene and the anticipation of the next—is appearing right now, on the same screen. The screen itself is not moving through time.

It is not stuck between scenes. It is the space in which every scene appears and disappears. In the same way, what you call "the past" is a memory appearing now. What you call "the future" is a thought appearing now. Both arise in the same field of awareness. So, the present is not a thin slice between two things. It is more like the open space of the screen itself—the timeless field in which all experiences of time show up.

Here's another way to feel this directly. Think about something that happened yesterday. Notice how it appears—as an image, a thought, maybe a feeling. Where is it appearing? Not in the past.

It's appearing now.

Now, imagine something that might happen tomorrow. That also appears as a thought… also now.

So, what we call "past" and "future" are not places we travel to. They are movements within this present field, which the mind describes as "past" or "future." And this field—this awareness—is not moving. It is not becoming. It is simply allowing everything to appear within it.

Modern neuroscience suggests that the brain does not perceive time directly; it constructs it. What we experience as the flow of time is simply the mind stitching together discrete sensory snapshots and organizing them into a narrative sequence. This "timeline" is useful for survival but has no independent reality outside cognition.

Quantum physics pushes this further, showing that, at the most fundamental level of existence, time is not a smooth river but an emergent property of observation. Events do not unfold in a strict linear order until they are measured or perceived. Wherever the light of awareness shines, that appears, lasts, and disappears. The point of observation determines time.

When viewed through the lens of Advaita Vedānta, all of this scientific evidence points back to the ancient insight that time belongs only to the mind, not to consciousness itself, which science now echoes. Through the practice of neti neti, one sees that neither memory (the past) nor anticipation (the future) can be the Self, as both are merely thoughts arising in awareness, which is neti. In the absence of identification with these mental movements, the apparent flow of time dissolves into the unmoving presence of the witness.

Remember, the witness never moves. It cannot look behind its own eyes. It just is. (Revisit the practice of neti neti in the previous chapter, if needed). Through it, past and future are revealed to be conceptual overlays only, and even the "present moment" is recognized as a thought about now, not the Now itself.

The Self, as pure awareness, stands outside time entirely—eternal not because it lasts forever, but because it does not participate in the temporal illusion at all. Concepts like "eternal" or "lasting" are just words that are useful in the limited linear timeframe; in true reality of the Self, however, those terms do not exist. In this recognition, the whole architecture of time collapses, leaving only the open, timeless field in which all appearances come and go without ever touching what you truly are: pure consciousness that just witnesses the play of its own energies going on within itself.

This chapter has probably been the hardest to follow and understand. I completely get it, as I was there once myself, struggling with the concept of letting go of the "I," abandoning the sense of control and responsibility, and relaxing in pure being once and for all.

It may take you some time to fully live this realization, as reading or hearing about it is just the first step, and one has to live it in practice to come into it fully. Again, it takes a healthy sense of logic, earnestness, honesty, and complete dedication and attention to live this nondual experience, to "kill" the you-possessor once and for all, and to start living life in freedom and enjoyment.

If you don't possess those five qualities, you will not be able to fully grasp this. If you do, then make this your number-one priority in life. Dedicate as much time daily as you can to practicing what I will offer you below. Trust me: making this your number-one priority in life is worth it. It's a chance that only a few get, and out of those few, even fewer succeed in attaining. But those who do will live a life devoid of suffering, conflict, and negative thoughts and built on complete inner peace.

Does the thought of never having to suffer again appeal to you? If yes, then make God number-one in your life, and the rest will follow.

At first, your ego will revolt—it will come up with everything and anything to distract you from killing it. But if you remain dedicated and committed, it will slowly ease its grasp and start letting go. That's why it's essential to stay with it. In fact, you may even get so angry after reading this chapter, you'll call it garbage and throw this book away—that's how strongly the ego may grasp to existence.

However, once you learn the truth, you cannot unlearn it, and your true nature will eventually come around to finding a way back to this knowledge and practices. No matter how the process unfolds within your individuality, do not judge it, do not beat yourself up, and most importantly, don't force yourself into any of it, as those are all done by the ego, and it will only draw you further away from your realization.

Chapter 5

Practices to Integrate the Teaching

ONCE YOU MAKE THIS Teaching and God your number-one priority, if simply reading and processing the material outlined in the previous chapters is not enough to fully start living this knowledge, then you should implement a set of practices offered below. They will help with shifting awareness and attention from constantly living in the ego-thoughts to just being present as your true being and, eventually, to complete realization of your true Self.

The first few practices I recommend here are for those who are so engrossed in the imaginary/mental world, they don't "live in the body" so to speak; they do not notice the physical world, which is God's most dense manifestation. If you find yourself constantly in your thoughts, unable to focus on just being present, start here. Dedicate at least five to ten minutes, twice a day to this, and you will begin to notice a huge difference.

Attuning to the Body

The goal of this practice is to shift attention from the mental/imaginary activity of description and possession to the physical presence of just being the body. The awareness will shift from "my body" and "my thoughts" to "I am the body present in the moment," which will allow you to shift to the first dense layer of God (refer to the Pyramid of Manifestation above).

Awareness of the body can be practiced in any everyday activity. The practice can be done anywhere and in any posture—standing, sitting, lying down, walking, or during ordinary daily routines. It is especially effective during simple, habitual actions.

The key principle is always the same: shift attention from thoughts into bodily sensations. Begin by becoming aware of your breathing without trying to control it. Simply feel how the body breathes on its own.

For example, during daily activities, such as while brushing your teeth, feel the brush touching your teeth and gums. Notice the taste of the toothpaste. Try switching hands (for example, brushing with your left if you are right-handed); this increases concentration and brings more attention into the body.

While showering, pull attention out of the mind, and focus on the sensation of water on skin. Feel the temperature of the water. Notice the scent of the shampoo or soap. Allow yourself to feel the body's contact with the water instead of performing the routine automatically.

When walking, sense how your foot touches the floor, ground, or pavement. Feel the pressure of the feet against the surface. Notice the sensation of clothing on your body, the collar on your neck. If there is wind, feel it moving through your hair.

When sitting, feel the weight of your body against the chair or sofa. Notice how the tongue rests against the palate. Sense how your back is supported by the surface behind you.

The essential instruction is to keep asking yourself throughout the day: "What is my body feeling right now?" Then, direct your attention directly to that sensation.

Deepening the Awareness of the Body

The next stage is shifting perception from "this is my body" to "I am the body." The goal is to start stepping out of automatic thinking into awareness of the physical body; feeling presence in the "here and now"; recognizing the body as a natural instrument of direct experience; and developing grounded, non-conceptual awareness of reality

Sit somewhere quiet. Close your eyes, and gently touch any part of the body—your hand, face, or leg.

Say internally, "This organism is called 'I.'" Then look at any object around you and say, "This phenomenon is called [object]."

I recommend getting mala beads for this practice—you can perform the below sequence exactly 108 times, sifting the beads one by one.

Alternate these statements, as you sift through the beads one by one:

- "This organism is called I - this phenomenon is called a tree."
- "This organism is called I - this phenomenon is called coffee."
- "This organism is called I - this phenomenon is called a car."
- "This organism is called I - this phenomenon is called a cloud."

This practice shifts attention away from mental concepts into direct embodied experience. When attention stabilizes in bodily sensations, the mind slows down, and perception becomes clearer and more vivid.

By the time you get to the 108th bead, your mind will be completely clear, and you will be fully present in the being of the current moment.

From Mental Description to Direct Perception

One of the most powerful ways to step out of the mind is to shift from describing life to perceiving it directly. Much of our experience is filtered through internal commentary—thoughts about what is happening rather than contact with what is actually happening. Yet life itself unfolds not in the mind but in the immediacy of sensation: sound, sight, smell, taste, and touch. The next foundational practice trains attention to return to this raw, unmediated reality by moving through the five gates of perception.

Begin by choosing a simple object or phenomenon around you: a cup of coffee, the sound of birds, the movement of air, the scent of perfume, or the feeling of fabric against the skin. Any object of the senses can serve as a portal back into the present moment. Once chosen, guide your awareness through each of the five sensory gates—sight, touch, smell, taste, and hearing— allowing perception to widen and deepen without mental analysis.

Start with vision. Look at the object before you, not merely to see it but to see into it. Notice its color, its texture, the way light reflects off its surface, and the movement or stillness that defines its form. Instead of thinking, *this is a cup,* experience the way sunlight plays across the porcelain. In this moment, the world reveals itself without interpretation. The mind is silent, and that's how the present moment truly shines!

Then, shift awareness to touch. Sense the object directly, or feel the sensations within your own body. Notice temperature, pressure, texture, moisture—sensations that arise without needing names. A warm cup in your hands becomes a direct, living encounter rather than an abstract idea.

Move next into smell. Gently inhale, and allow the aroma to reveal itself without categorizing or evaluating. Experience it as pure sensation: the bitter fragrance of coffee, the sweetness of soap, the freshness of air. Let attention dwell in the subtlety of scent without moving into thought.

If you are drinking or eating, explore taste. Sense the layers of flavor, the warmth, the subtle shifts as the taste evolves on the tongue. Taste becomes a landscape of sensation—alive, shifting, immediate.

Finally, open to sound. Listen to the noises around you: wind, voices, footsteps, distant hums. Do not judge them as pleasant or unpleasant. Hear them the way a river might hear itself—simply waves of sound arising and falling. When listening becomes pure receptivity, the mind begins to soften and expand.

As attention moves through these gates, something profound happens: perception becomes direct. Experience unfolds without commentary. You shift from thinking about the world to being with the world. This opens the doorway to presence in a way that is simple, natural, and immediately accessible.

Repeat this cycle three to five times in a row, either with the same object or with different ones. Each repetition strengthens the bridge from conceptual thinking to true sensory experience. With practice, awareness deepens; the familiar world becomes fresh, vivid, and intimate.

The results are transformative. You begin to recognize yourself not as a thinker describing reality but as awareness perceiving it directly. Filters fall away. Presence expands. Sensory clarity sharpens. You rediscover the world as it is—not as the mind imagines it to be.

The underlying insight emerges with simplicity and power: We do not live in reality itself. We live in our mental description of it. And remember from the neuroscientific research above, the description always lags and has nothing to do with the present moment of reality as it truly is. But reality is always here, and we can return to it at any moment through the five gates of perception.

The next set of practices is for you to try when you've mastered being present in the body, the senses, and the direct experience of reality through simple awareness, not in the mental/imaginary world.

Becoming Aware of Space and the Silent Field of Perception

As awareness expands through deconcentrating on the mental processes and living in simple being, a subtle yet transformative shift becomes possible: the movement from perceiving objects to perceiving the space in which objects appear. In ordinary perception, attention is drawn to forms—sounds, sensations, thoughts, colors—and rarely notices the vast, silent backdrop that makes perception possible. Yet space is always present, unchanging, and intimately felt when attention becomes soft and panoramic (remember our initial discussion in Chapter 1 on how this void space is the foundation of everything that appears in it). This foundational practice guides you into awareness of this spaciousness, gradually revealing that the "observer" is not separate from the field of experience but arises within it.

Begin by opening your attention to the room around you. Do not focus on the walls, furniture, or any specific object. Instead, sense the volume of the room—the openness, the air, the emptiness between things. Feel how sound echoes within the space, how the body occupies it, how breath moves through it.

As you relax into this awareness, you may notice that the space behind you becomes just as vivid as the space in front of you. Awareness ceases to be a narrow beam and becomes a spherical presence—surrounding, enveloping, boundless. Imagine it as if you had a powerful microscope, where boundaries of each shape are blurred into one vibrating field of space.

This shift into spatial awareness naturally reduces the mind's tendency to cling to objects. The world becomes less about what you are looking at and more about the field in which looking occurs. Sensations arise within the space of the body; sounds arise within the space of the room; thoughts arise within the space of awareness itself. When attention recognizes space as part of perception, the grip of identification begins to loosen.

(A few years back I used to listen to Kryon, an inter-dimensional being channeled by an American scientist. Although channeling and beings dissolve in the knowledge of the ultimate truth, some of their teachings are useful for shifting awareness internally while attaining it. Kryon used to say the space between the tiniest particles that modern-day science is able to identify is God itself. He would refer to it as the God-force that makes the particles actually appear/move. I was unable to understand this statement fully until I found this Teaching, but now, I find it a perfect complement to this practice).

From here, explore the subtle "gap" between experiences. After a sound ends, before the next sensation appears, in the quiet pause between exhalation and inhalation, there is a moment of stillness. It is not the absence of experience but the presence of pure awareness.

This gap is always here, though often unnoticed. As you become sensitive to it, you begin to sense awareness not as a doing but as a silent background against which life unfolds. That awareness is the space and is God and is you. What you previously assumed to be "you" begins to appear as a series of sensations and thoughts occurring inside a vast, unmoving presence.

This recognition deepens when you turn attention toward the sense of "I" itself—the inner position from which you believe you are observing the world. Ask yourself: *Where is this observer located? Is it in the head? Behind the eyes? In the chest?*

Notice that "I" cannot be found as a fixed point. Instead, it feels more like a subtle tension, a contraction in the field of awareness. Sit with this contraction. Allow it to be seen, not resisted.

As you observe the sense of "I," something remarkable occurs: it begins to dissolve, not through force but through recognition. You realize that the observer is not a solid entity but another appearance within awareness, just like sounds, sensations, or thoughts. The one who seems to be "looking" is actually part of the picture, not separate from it.

Awareness is looking at itself through the illusion of an observer. The observer has to exist for awareness to be able to look at itself, but you find, in this practice and the chapters leading up to it, that the content of the observation is non-dual of the observer or the space where the observation occurs—you cannot take the observer out of the space where the observation occurs. They are one.

Once this is seen, even briefly, a profound relaxation arises. You no longer need to control experience or divide it into inner and outer. Everything—sensations, space, thoughts, the sense of self—appears within a single, unified field of awareness. You begin to sense that awareness is not in the body; the body is in awareness. Space is not outside you; you are the spaciousness in which space appears.

This stage marks the beginning of a deeper unfolding: the recognition that the ego, the "I"-center, is not the perceiver but a fleeting ripple in the vastness of consciousness. The practices that follow will deepen this insight, guiding you toward a stable understanding of yourself as the silent, open field in which all of life arises and dissolves.

Neti Neti

The above practice of becoming aware of space, along with neti neti, which was discussed previously, will fully release awareness from the "I-doer." I won't restate the neti neti here, as it was already discussed, but practicing it was transformational on my own journey, and I consider it key in the search of the Self.

Expanding Awareness Beyond Body

As concentration deepens and the sense of spacious perception stabilizes, a natural shift occurs: awareness begins to expand beyond the boundaries of the physical body. We are so used to self-identifying with the body, but when you practice the awareness of space as one field, where everything including the body occurs spontaneously and by no one's doing, you will see that what was once experienced as "my" body—this skin, these sensations—begins to feel less like a container and more like a localized expression within a much wider field.

The next foundational practice guides you through this transition, revealing the subtle movement from "I am aware" to "awareness is aware."

To begin, sit comfortably with your eyes closed, and let your attention rest in the body without focusing on any particular point. Instead of honing in on sensations, allow them to exist as part of a wider field.

Sense the breath, the posture, the quiet pulse of aliveness—but sense them as ripples, not as separate events. In this state, the body becomes porous, almost transparent. It is no longer a solid object but a constellation of sensations floating in awareness.

From here, begin to notice the space around the body. Feel the air touching your skin, the volume of space above your head, the space behind your back, the subtle emptiness surrounding your hands and feet. Gradually, allow this spatial awareness to become just as vivid as the awareness of physical sensation.

As you soften into this openness, the distinction between "body" and "space" becomes less defined. The body seems to dissolve into the space, and the space seems to permeate the body. Perception grows spherical, all-directional.

Go back to the idea that your body is made of this space—remember the powerful microscope that shows how we are all part of the same vibrating field of energy. In this practice, you start actually experiencing this, not just theoretically knowing it.

When this openness stabilizes, turn your attention to the process of awareness itself. Instead of thinking, "I am aware of the space," notice how the experience unfolds effortlessly. Space is perceived without the need for a perceiver. Sounds arise without the need for a listener. Awareness does not belong to "someone"; it is simply present.

This shift is subtle yet profound—the core transition from personal "doership" to impersonal witnessing.

As awareness becomes impersonal, emotional patterns and contractions naturally rise to the surface. Old tensions—fear, anger, grief, or tightness in the chest or throat—may appear as condensed pockets within the spacious field. Rather than resisting them, allow these contractions to be held within the openness of awareness. See them not as "my emotions" but as energetic ripples appearing within the same space that holds breath, sensation, and sound.

This gentle inclusion dissolves resistance and reveals that even emotional suffering is simply movement within awareness—not a flaw in the self, but a temporary wave in the ocean of experience

(Eventually, you will be able to go even deeper and realize, if you remove the labels "fear," "anger," "grief" from the energetic ripples, they lose any meaning of power over you completely and are just witnessed by you in the moment they appear. Experiencing without labeling anything with language liberates one completely.)

Over time, something even more subtle emerges: the intuitive recognition that the sense of "I"—the observer you believed yourself to be—is not actually perceiving anything. It is itself perceived. It appears as a faint contraction, a habit of identification, a small knot of attention claiming ownership over what arises. When observed clearly, this "I-sense" loses its solidity and becomes transparent. It dissolves back into the field of awareness, revealing a profound simplicity:

There is perception, but no perceiver.

There is awareness, but no one who is aware.

This dissolution of the observer is not an annihilation but a liberation. The weight of having to manage experience falls away. The world is no longer filtered through a center that must judge, control, interpret, or resist. Instead, life reveals itself as an unbroken, spontaneous unfolding occurring in a vast, centerless presence.

As the sense of "I" begins to fade, awareness becomes expansive, effortless, and deeply peaceful. Experience continues—sounds, sensations, thoughts—but without a personal anchor. What remains is a spacious, intimate field in which everything arises and disappears.

This is not a mystical trance or an altered state. It is a return to the natural condition of consciousness when it is not burdened by identification.

Dark and Silent Retreat

When the sense of "I" is mostly exhausted or set aside as "not me," one can practice the gradual withdrawal of attention from sensory perception.

In ordinary experience, awareness is constantly tied to objects—things we see, hear, touch, smell, and taste. Even when the mind is quiet, perception usually remains object-oriented. If you can master the practices of widening awareness beyond objects and becoming aware of space, as the above practices teach, the culmination of the foundational practices invites a deeper retreat, one in which sensory input is minimized and awareness is allowed to recognize itself directly, without intermediaries.

My Teacher Pasha, would invite one to practice a dark retreat: a complete immersion in darkness and silence, not as an extreme technique, but as a natural extension of the earlier practices. For this practice, one has to spend a few days alone, in the dark, with no sensory distractions.

Please be aware: this retreat is *not* for the untrained mind and definitely *not* for someone who is just in the beginning stages of the spiritual journey. Consciousness ready for this kind of experience enters it effortlessly, so please do not force yourself into any practices, especially this one.

In the dark and silent retreat, when visual input is removed, when sound is reduced to near silence, when taste and smell are absent, and when speech ceases entirely, attention no longer has external objects to grasp. The nervous system begins to settle, and perception turns inward on its own. Fasting or consuming only water with lemon may accompany this retreat, not as an act of discipline but as a gentle detoxification on all levels—physical, mental, and perceptual.

As the senses withdraw, familiar reference points dissolve. There are no images to see, no sounds to follow, no smells or tastes to engage. Even bodily sensations, at first vivid, gradually soften and fade. What remains is not emptiness in a negative sense, but a quiet, transparent presence. Awareness begins to notice itself not through contrast, but through continuity. When attention no longer feeds perception, it naturally recognizes its own nature.

Thoughts may still arise at first, often intensifying as the mind searches for something to hold onto. The instruction here is simple and precise: do not fight thoughts, and do not engage them. Thoughts are just uninvited guests. If they are neither entertained nor resisted, they eventually leave on their own. One by one, mental images dissolve. Inner dialogue quiets. The sense of time loosens. What remains is a clear, spacious awareness, like transparent water—present, still, and self-luminous.

In this state, if attained, a crucial realization stabilizes: thoughts are not produced by a thinker. They arise spontaneously and disappear in the same way. You do not choose the next thought, cannot predict it, and cannot stop it through force. When this is seen clearly, the illusion of control collapses. The mind loses its authority not through suppression, but through understanding. Awareness remains, unchanged and untroubled.

As this recognition deepens, the distinction between awareness and space dissolves. Space is no longer perceived as an external container, but as an aspect of awareness itself. Emptiness, space, and knowing are revealed as three expressions of the same reality. You begin to experience yourself not as a body within space, nor as a mind observing experience, but as the open field in which all phenomena arise and vanish.

This retreat marks the completion of the foundational practices. You may notice that what began as attention to bodily sensation unfolds into a direct recognition of awareness as the ground of all experience. The sense of a separate observer fades. The need to control or interpret life falls away. Perception continues, but without a center, the doer, the actor, the chooser. Life happens, but no one is "doing" it.

When engaged in these practices with honesty and earnestness, you will realize:

- ✧ You are not your thoughts.
- ✧ You are not your sensations.
- ✧ You are not the one who perceives.
- ✧ You are the awareness in which perceiving happens.

With this recognition, practice is no longer something you do. It becomes the way life is lived—open, immediate, and free from the burden of a separate self. The practices do not lead to something new; they reveal what has always been present, waiting only to be noticed.

Chapter 6

Concept 3 of the Teaching: Effortless Manifestation

IF YOU'VE MADE IT to this chapter or simply skipped the rest to find out how to manifest your desires, I want to stop you and ask a question: are "you" still here?

The individual Joe, Jane, or whatever the name is, *Are you still there?* Are "you" looking to fulfill "your" wishes, to receive confirmation, approval, or other social benefits that will come with the attainment of those wishes?

If the answer is "yes," I don't want you to read this chapter. Not because it is a secret available only to the enlightened ones, but because any attempt to manifest from the ego will always end up in failure. Even if your wishes come true, you will end up chasing the next shiny object or contrasting your achievements with those of others, becoming a slave to the ego who will never stop desiring.

That's why the complete death of "you" is required to enter effortless manifestation. If you are not quite there yet, please go back to the previous chapters and spend most of your time dedicating attention to the practices outlined in Chapter 5, above. Remember, it takes time. It took me almost two years, but the time will vary from person to person, depending on how strong the grip of the ego identity is on the pyramid of your individual realization.

Please, give yourself time. Be honest, earnest, and present, and make God your number-one priority.

If, on the other hand, you read the opening paragraph and answered back, "Who's me? I don't know who Joe/Jane/your name is!" then please, read on. Happy manifesting!

True Manifesting is Altruism

Imagine waking up one day and realizing you are the only person left on the planet. Everyone else has vanished, leaving all mansions, cars, money, food, and stores with all kinds of goods open and available to you alone. Would you go to those stores? Make an effort to put on your best clothes and makeup? Would you move money and goods from one house to the other when you are the only one left to use all of them?

See, true manifesting does not arise from the ego's wanting, because the ego always manifests from lack. It seeks something for a separate fragment, measured against other fragments, and therefore remains trapped in comparison and scarcity. But if you are the only fragment that's left, will you seek that comparison? And will there ever be scarcity?

What arises from realization of the Teaching discussed in this book is fundamentally different. When awareness recognizes itself as already whole, absolute, and complete, there is nothing left to acquire. If you are everything, then what can you possibly lack? What remains is the natural movement of giving away from yourself. That is the true mechanism of creation. This is how creation of the universe itself unfolds, not as a desire to possess, but as an overflow of fullness.

The Absolute/God exploded with a Big Bang, manifesting itself into billions of particles, which then shaped into elements, which in turn shaped into planets and stars and, finally, into living objects. Isn't that altruism? The Absolute does not manifest to gain; it manifests by sharing itself as form. Every world, every body, every moment, and every form appears as a generosity of being, a being that creates out of its own fullness or absolute potential.

Altruism is an expression of wholeness rather than a strategy for improvement. When action flows from this place, it does not compete or extract; it serves, supports, and sustains the whole. What appears in the world then is not "my manifestation," but life responding to life, abundance moving where there is openness, and form arising as a natural extension of what is already complete. Form that will last and disappear back into its origin—the absolute potential nothingness.

My dear Teacher Pasha used this analogy. Imagine an island made entirely of gold. The ground, the trees, the mountains, and the air shimmering in the heat—everything is gold. Now, imagine a figure standing on that island who wishes to manifest gold.

The wish itself is paradoxical, because the one who wants is already made of gold, standing on gold, and surrounded by gold. Nothing new can be added. The only thing that can happen is that gold reshapes itself, appearing as a ring, say, or a cup, a statue, a doorway. The substance never changes; only the form does.

In the same way, when manifestation flows from realization, it is not an attempt to acquire something missing, but instead is a creative reshaping of what already is, which is all you. Awareness does not produce from desire, but from play. It does not manifest *for* itself, because it already is everything; it manifests *as* itself, taking on forms that nourish, support, and express the whole. When this is seen, manifesting stops being a personal act of wanting and becomes a universal movement of generosity: life forming itself into new shapes, simply because it can, with pure and unconditional love for all there is, as all is itself.

In both Advaita and Dzogchen Buddhism, there are teachings that speak of vast creative capacities arising once identification with the personal self has dissolved. Monks and realized practitioners are not described as manifesting from desire or ambition, but from freedom, participating consciously in the creative play of the Absolute itself.

In Dzogchen, this is sometimes expressed as awareness effortlessly displaying worlds, realms, and forms within its own luminous expanse, while in Advaita it appears as lila, the divine play in which Brahman (the Absolute) takes shape without ever becoming divided. (Līlā in Sanskrit means "divine play" or "cosmic game." In Advaita and broader Hindu philosophy, it describes the way the Absolute (Brahman) appears as the universe not out of necessity, lack, or purpose, but out of freedom, creativity, and delight.)

These manifestations are not pursued to secure identity, status, or power. The practitioner does not become a ruler instead of being whole; the role of ruler, creator, or guardian appears as a costume worn lightly by wholeness itself.

Just as a child might play every role in an imagined world without confusion about who they are, realization allows creation to unfold as a creative game rather than a strategy for fulfillment. Nothing is gained; nothing is owned. Forms arise, dissolve, and arise again, while awareness remains untouched. In this way, manifestation becomes an act of expression rather than acquisition, a spontaneous movement of the Absolute delighting in its own infinite capacity to appear.

How does this happen, practically speaking? Once you find yourself as pure consciousness with no separation or borders, your human life does not stop; it continues on, along with feelings, thoughts, and actions. You learn to not possess those, but they continue—effortlessly, without a doer or controller. However, the personality, or the form of the absolute that carries your name, still lives in a certain point of view—like our planet in the vast expanse of space with billions of other planets. And that point of view shapes what manifests around it.

When you realize your true nature, manifestation becomes the true altruism. Not in the sense that you give away all your worldly possessions, but in the sense where everything manifests out of you. God gives itself away by manifesting physical reality, so any inclination, desire, or wish arising in this conscious presence manifests effortlessly just by pure nature of how things are created.

It is very important again here to understand that this manifestation does not belong to anyone; there is no "doer" or "manifestor" whose wishes magically come true. The moment he/she appears, manifestation becomes a struggle of achievement and disappointment. Fear, hope, worry, anxiety, and excitement all creep in to disrupt the natural flow of things and affect the outcome.

In the absence of the doer, however, there can be no fear or other emotions, as no one is left to be afraid for the outcome. The desire becomes like a seed that hits the fertile quantum field of potential and sprouts into being without anything stunting its growth. The true power of this manifestation is truly only felt when the vampire of the ego that doubts, questions, fears, and hopes is completely destroyed.

Manifesting in Business

By way of example, after the Teaching entered my life and I dedicated all of my free time and energy into practicing, living, and breathing it, all of "my" old desires magically came true in ways I never anticipated.

Before, there was the overachiever attorney and business owner, who felt the need to constantly control every process, every step, and every move, in fear that something would be missed. What resulted was that my path was always laid with multiple obstacles and every fear I had manifested itself into those obstacles. When the controller went to forever rest in peace, along with the owner, the doer, the achiever, and their extended family, ridden with constant contradictory emotions and feelings, everything started happening effortlessly, naturally, and oh-so beautifully.

For years, I ran my law firm as a controlling overachiever—I set goals; I struggled to reach them; I hired different business coaches; I hired different marketing agencies; I made mistakes and persevered. Although all of those sound like regular things any business owner has to do, what really matters is the position or the state you are in when doing all of those things. From the ego-based mentality, I was always reaching, nothing was ever enough, nothing worked quite as I expected, and the goals were never quite achieved.

As I said before, the ego always has one "ideal" option it considers as an acceptable variation of how things should unfold, and it sets that "ideal" as its goal. In reality, things unfold unexpectedly and beautifully without anyone controlling the outcome, and when the unfolding does not coincide with the ideal outcome of the ego's goal, a whole slew of emotions unfolds—disappointment, self-punishment, failure, blame, guilt, etc. These emotions rattle the consequent unfolding and manifest reality that is chaotic and always in the carrot/stick cycle. That is how the ego thrives and continues existing.

And that is how I approached my business until I found the Teaching. I had financial goals, marketing goals, client goals, etc., But whenever one of them didn't pan out, I would collapse into overanalyzing, taking chaotic actions, and blaming myself for never getting it "right." My firm still grew year to year, and I continued to appear successful (as that is how 95% of all business owners operate), but I was constantly stressed, worried, and overrun by competing thoughts and ideas, always doubting my decisions and worrying about the next month/quarter/year.

When I truly internalized the Teaching, however, this pattern shifted. When the ego-doer dissolves in God, God creates without obstruction. Seen through a modern lens of a business owner in my example, this is a shift from local control to field intelligence.

The ego behaves like a classical object, believing causality runs through force and personal will. But reality moves more like a quantum field—non-local, relational, responsive. When interference collapses, coherence appears. Action arises without strain. Decisions crystallize the way particles do when measurement stops distorting the system. What remains is not passivity, but precision.

This is why surrender of the "I" is not the enemy of effectiveness, but its precondition. The ego attempts to collapse possibility through anxiety, gripping timelines, outcomes, and identity. The field responds with friction. When the fictional controller (business owner) relaxes, possibility organizes itself. God/the field self-expresses. In practical terms, like business, leadership, and creation, work gets done with less noise, less drag, and fewer self-inflicted obstacles. Effort decreases. Alignment increases. Results follow, not because the ego-self tried harder, but because it finally stopped getting in the way.

When I stopped worrying or controlling and dissolved into God/the field, my firm started having its best months ever. Instead of counting leads and worrying, I surrendered into letting God take over and only taking the precise actions that were necessary.

My Teacher Pasha, calls this action-taking the "working intelligence." This intelligence does not belong to anyone. It is God's tool, but it takes the precise needed action when the right circumstance requires it to. When the working intelligence is clear and not muddled by conflicting thoughts and emotions, it naturally acts harmoniously and achieves the best results by following the path of least resistance. That, again, is physics.

In physics, interference degrades coherence. The more variables you force into a system—e.g., noise, fear, anticipation, self-protection—the more energy is lost to friction. When interference drops, systems naturally reorganize into more efficient states. By surrendering control, I wasn't abandoning action; I was removing the distortions that were obscuring it.

It is not personal. It does not belong to the individual mind, personality, or ego. In physics terms, it is not a localized operator, but a field effect. The same intelligence that organizes electrons into stable orbitals or causes fluids to follow paths of least resistance operates here. When conditions are clear, action happens exactly when needed—and only then. No excess motion. No wasted energy. No compulsive activity masquerading as productivity.

Importantly, it wasn't only fear and doubt that interfered with the field. Positive emotions did, as well. Hope, excitement, anticipation, even the sense of achievement all subtly presuppose a future self who will be allowed to feel them once a desired outcome arrives. That assumption reinstates the very doer that surrender dissolves.

In physical terms, this is still interference: an early collapse of the system around imagined reward. The field responds not to optimism or despair, but to coherence. Emotional investment, whether pleasant or painful, introduces bias, pulling energy out of the present configuration and into projection. When even the desire to feel successful fell away, action became sharper and timing more exact. What remained was neutral clarity. From that neutrality, the working intelligence could operate without distortion, unclaimed by anyone, uncolored by outcome—again, following the same principles by which physical systems minimize resistance and conserve energy.

This surrender to God/the field reshaped "me" from an overachiever who operates chaotically out of worry and hope, into God's tool. My working intelligence now runs a firm· that is successful, harmonious, and produces the highest-quality legal work in the estate planning field. Since my "death," the firm doubled its number of five-star client reviews in less than a year (where it took four years to get the prior half); doubled the number of leads; has the best team of employees who work as a cohesive family unit; and brings me the greatest sense of fulfillment I could ever have dreamed of.

Manifesting in Relationships

In my personal life and relationships, when the Teaching was finally lived rather than understood, that controlling structure dissolved. What died was the internal manager who needed resistance in order to feel real. The contrasting with "others"—my dad, other family members, etc.,—was no longer necessary; and without contrasting, those relationships naturally harmonized.

In its absence, working intelligence could operate without obstruction. This intelligence does not strategize reconciliation or negotiate outcomes; it responds to conditions. Without emotional interference, such as defensiveness, blame, anticipation, or anger, the personality equipped with the working intelligence acts precisely. Words come when needed. Silence appears when more functional than speech. There was no effort to repair the relationship with my father, and because of that, repair occurred. The system found its own equilibrium.

This is how God/field coherence expresses itself in human relationships. When interference at one node collapses, the entire relational field reorganizes. My father did not need to change first. No one needed to be convinced, forgiven, or understood. The removal of resistance was sufficient, as the resistance always comes from the ego. ("My Dad wronged me," "He should have apologized," "My parents mistreated me," etc.)

Conversations softened naturally, as there was no proving the point to the "other." Tension dissipated without explanation, where we became one divine play of energies instead of two separate clashing illusions. What remained was alignment, not reconciliation as an act of will, since the possessor of the will died and finally left everything as it should be.

The same working intelligence when acting naturally and unintentionally within God/field resolved other distortions. Toxic friendships dissolved without drama, because they required egoic feedback loops to survive. When those loops were gone, there was nothing for them to attach to. New relationships appeared not through seeking, but through resonance. I completely replaced my friend circle, not through effort or fights and drama, but by just the natural falling away of what was no longer useful.

My current friendships are fulfilling, harmonious, and filled with love, joy, and mutual respect. Friendships that were tense, superficial, or driven by ego-centric tendencies simply ended without any effort or purposeful actions. New clients gravitated toward the firm not because of branding or persuasion, but because coherence attracts coherence. In a field governed by least resistance, energy flows toward clarity. People respond to the absence of distortion the way physical systems respond to reduced friction.

Working intelligence is not personal, emotional, or relational in the human sense. It is systemic. Once the egoic controller steps aside, the field handles calibration everywhere at once: family, friendships, business, and community. Nothing is managed. Nothing is forced. Alignment propagates automatically.

This, again, is not just spirituality applied to life. It is also physics observed through living systems. When the "I-doer" collapses and you find yourself as one with everything there is, the simple proven laws of physics apply to everything there is, as nothing is creating a resisting node to obstruct the natural flow of energies.

I have to caution you here, as sometimes this is misunderstood, and the new "spiritually-awakened" ego is born and replaces the old by trying to let go of drama and emotions. But the spiritually-awakened self is still the self that is separate and lives in contrast with the others. It is very important to distinguish when this effort takes place.

This also does not mean that you now are in a permanent state of bliss, emotional numbness, or spiritual detachment. Emotions still arise. Anger, sadness, frustration, joy, and tenderness move through the system as natural responses to life and as temperamental tendencies of a particular body-mind/personality. The difference is not their absence, but the absence of ownership.

When emotions are no longer claimed as mine, they leave no residue. They do not harden into identity, accumulate into grievance, or spin into recurring conflict. Without a center to orbit, they pass the way clouds pass through open sky. This is why karma loses its grip: not because reactions stop, but because nothing is stored. What remains is a natural flow of response, expression, and resolution, unobstructed by memory, narrative, or self-protection. The emotions are not treated as "good" or "bad"; they simply are, as everything else is—in its own place, perfect, without the need to control or change anything.

I still yell at my kids when they piss me off; I still argue when the opponent makes no sense; I still root for my son's soccer team and scream out profanities when they lose. But I don't judge myself for doing that; I don't cling to emotions; I don't hide my "shadow," which the New-Age therapists tell you to embrace. I simply surrender to God, dissolve in God, and actions/emotions/feelings come and go, with nothing to hold onto, as there is no one who could hold on.

As with anything else created in this God/field, human emotions, feelings, and experiences simply come and go, but the ego clings to them to create ongoing conflict, and that's where all mental disorders and other illnesses take place. The ocean does not become depressed after it manifested as a devastating storm; it simply carries on with calm; then storms again; then calms yet again. It does not lose its mind, thinking, "I caused the storm and the devastation, and I need to be blamed and punished." The ocean would be in a mental facility, and we would have no ocean left, if it had the ability to do what we humans do with our egos.

Similarly, the sky turns blue and calm after heavy clouds erupt with hail, rain, or snow. The clouds pass, and the sky appears calm and blue again. It does not try to "fix" the rain or assign blame for why it rained at a certain time and why over this or that particular geographical region.

Animals also do not get depressed because they were born carnivores, while others are herbivores. They don't start wars over whether being a carnivore or an herbivore is better or right. They don't self-blame for eating meat or grass; they don't judge themselves for gaining a few pounds while being pregnant, and they don't put on makeup or fancy clothes to look good to the others.

Do you see how only human egos distort all of this? In nature, there is no ego, no possessor, and thus no right or wrong. Things just are. Clouds come and go, waves come and go, days give way to nights, and flowers bloom and die. There is nobody judging whether any of that is somehow right or wrong, good or bad, timely or not. With humans possessing the highest level of intelligence, though, we created and started firmly believing in an illusion of this separate "doer" who decides what to label right, wrong, good, or bad.

If we just let those concepts go, we will flow in a beautiful and effortless way, just like the rest of the nature does. The laws of physics apply to all human emotions and manifestations, just like they apply to everything else in nature, but the ego attempts to distort the natural flow of things by trying to possess or control the laws of physics. Quite crazy, isn't it?

Again, this Teaching has nothing to do with psychology/therapy/self-help, etc., as all of those appeal to the ego, bolster it, and put cushions under its behind, to make sure it is comfortable existing in the delusions of the suffering beings. This does not describe repression or dissociation or any other disorder that the ego may be diagnosed with. Nothing is being pushed down, bypassed, or numbed.

In repression, emotion is suppressed and stored, remaining active beneath awareness; in dissociation, sensation is cut off entirely as a protective response to overwhelm. Both keep the nervous system locked in a stress loop. What is described here is completely different. Emotions still fully register in the body—anger tightens the chest, sadness softens the breath, fear sharpens attention. But they are not amplified by narrative or defended by identity.

From a neurological perspective, this reflects a system that can move fluidly between activation and resolution. The sympathetic response may engage, but it completes its cycle and returns to baseline instead of being prolonged by rumination or self-referential thinking, just as the sky goes back to being blue and calm after a thunderstorm passes through it.

Without ownership, emotion does not recruit the default-mode network into replay and anticipation; it resolves as sensation, not memory to hold on to and store. This is why no psychological residue remains. Reactions occur, but they are metabolized, let go, and replaced by new ones. The body responds, discharges, and resets. What looks like emotional freedom is simply a nervous system allowed to do what it was designed to do: respond, complete, and move on, without a fictional center insisting on holding the experience as mine.

When the experience is "mine," psychology, therapy, and other means of bolstering the illusion are utilized to shift nonexistent blame to some "other" beings or external circumstance. But having proven through personal experience of enlightenment discussed in this book that "external" or "other" does not exist and all is one awareness, the concepts of therapy become completely ridiculous and fall off. It's as if the pinkie finger went to therapy to resolve the drama of being the smallest and least useful, while blaming the thumb for its shortcomings.

Ludicrous, but that's how 99% of people, caught in the delusion of the ego, function.

Manifesting Desired Objects

When it comes to other types of manifesting, as in actual things you desire to have or a certain amount of money you need, the logic and the mechanism is still the same: complete peace and surrender to God, with just the working intelligence doing its job. Under the same logic, what we call *desire* stops being personal and starts being structural. A house, a car, a sum of money arise not as trophies for a self, but as configurations the field temporarily takes when conditions align.

Desire, when freed from ownership, is no longer craving—it becomes information. A seed placed into fertile soil does not strain to grow, and the soil does not ask for whom the tree will exist. In the same way, a wish held without attachment does not belong to anyone; it is simply a pattern introduced into the quantum field. When interference is absent, i.e., when there is no anxious claimant waiting to receive, the field organizes itself accordingly. Form appears because it can, not because someone demanded it.

What manifests is not possessed; it is participated in. Money moves, homes appear, and paths open, not as proof of worth or fulfillment of identity, but as expressions of lila, the divine play in which creation explores itself through endless forms, then lets them go again, unchanged at the source. Creation itself is not attached to the coming and going of the forms, as it is one and the same with all of them.

As an example, I always wanted to own a house by the beach. I love Colorado, but I do not tolerate cold very well, and the idea of having a warm place to escape to always appealed to me and warmed my heart. Every time I considered it, however, the mental and emotional bodies generated doubts: "Can I afford this? Where would I look? How difficult would it be to manage from a distance?"

In the past, those thoughts always collapsed into overplanning or paralysis. This time, the desire was allowed to remain impersonal—noticed but not claimed. The thought of a house was simply planted into the quantum field of potential.

Shortly after, a friend casually offered her home in Florida as a place to stay, while I was telling her about our upcoming trip to Universal Studios. While there, I toured a few houses with my kids, without urgency or expectation, then I left. Only later did the actual purchase occur—an offer made on a house I had never seen in person. It unfolded smoothly, not because of certainty, but because the system stayed coherent. As the natural flow of things unfolded, an opportunity presented itself, allowing working intelligence to operate at the field level and reorganize form without local interference.

Logistics, timing, and execution emerged precisely when needed, handled by the field rather than by anxious effort. What appeared was not something achieved, but something permitted. I love my house in Florida, but I have no sense of attachment or control or ownership over it. I simply enjoy going there, even though the work it took to furnish it and make it our second home would have discouraged any ego from ever considering owning one.

As another example, I always wanted to write a book. From my very early childhood into adolescence and then adulthood, I had various fiction and non-fiction ideas. I wrote short stories, essays, and poems, and I even started with a few chapters of various books I aspired to write.

But not a single one ever came to fruition, as the ego always found doubts and obstacles: "Would I get a lot of criticism? What if nobody likes my book? How would I find a publisher? How would I promote it? Would anyone even buy it? Would my family/friends judge me for writing a story that had nothing to do with my main professional practice?"

All of these thoughts kept me in a decades-long block, where ideas came and went, but none of them actually manifested into a published book, because the ego nipped them in the bud by imposing all of those doubts and fears.

A year after the Teaching permeated every aspect of my life, I was hosting an event for my firm, where we educate mothers of young children about the value of estate planning. One of the attendees came up to me after the event and expressed her fondness of the idea behind the event and her eagerness to create an estate plan. We clicked on a personal level immediately, chatted for a while, and I was very excited to help her plan her estate.

She scheduled an appointment, and when we met at my office a week later, she asked me in a casual conversation whether I'd ever considered writing a book. I was so surprised and excited to hear that question, I immediately told her about my efforts and aspirations, as well as what held me back. That lady was none other but the owner of Landon Hail Press, the publishing company that published this book you are now reading. After working on her estate plan, I became a client of her publishing house, and my aspirations to write a book finally manifested in an effortless, natural, extremely fulfilling, and beautiful way.

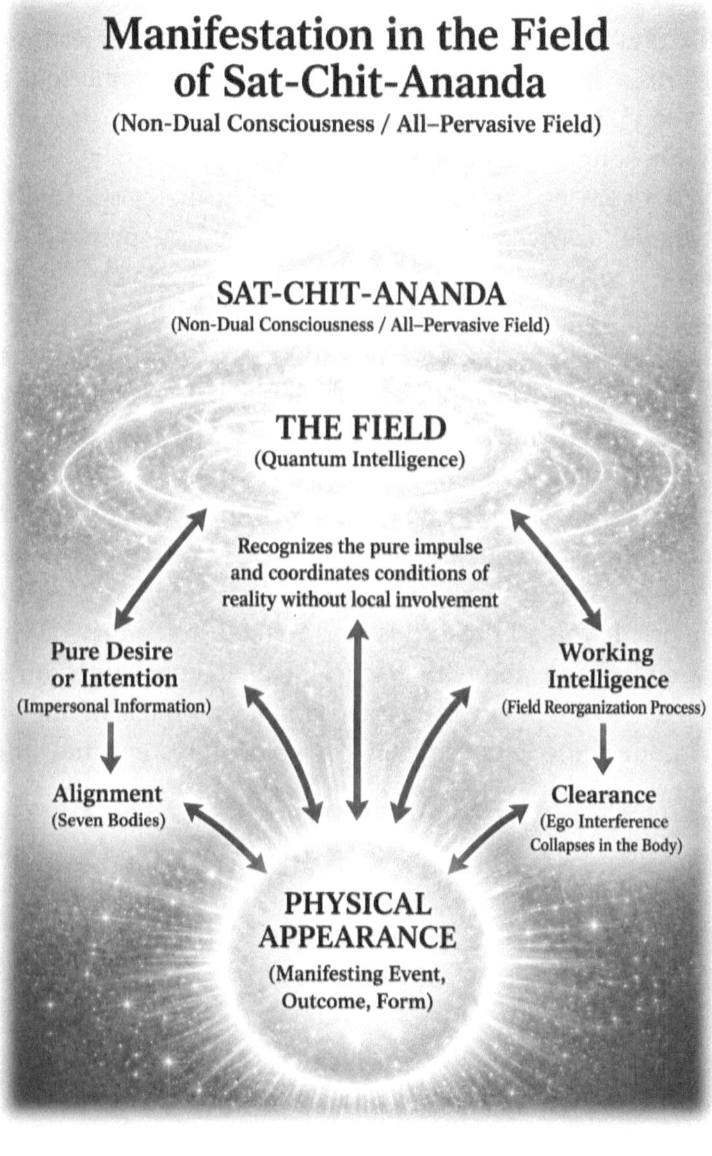
Manifestation in the Field
of Sat-Chit-Ananda
(Non-Dual Consciousness / All–Pervasive Field)
SAT-CHIT-ANANDA
(Non-Dual Consciousness / All–Pervasive Field)
THE FIELD
(Quantum Intelligence)
Recognizes the pure impulse
and coordinates conditions of
reality without local involvement
Pure Desire
or Intention
(Impersonal Information)
Working
Intelligence
(Field Reorganization Process)
Alignment
(Seven Bodies)
Clearance
(Ego Interference
Collapses in the Body)
PHYSICAL
APPEARANCE
(Manifesting Event,
Outcome, Form)

Remember our diagram of the Seven Bodies? The diagram on the prior page visually demonstrates how effortless manifestation happens through a simple tool of working intelligence, where the ego does not drain the manifesting energy into its constant chaotic chatter.

To sum up, any manifestation from the ego feels like struggle or overachieving, as the field responds with resistance based on the feelings and emotions you are transmitting. In order to truly manifest, the ego must completely fall off, and any desires cannot belong to anybody or be for somebody. Then, the Universe/God/field will arrange manifestation to take place in the most efficient, energy-saving, and harmonious way.

I would suggest not even reading the chapter on manifesting if you are not 100% clear on the previous chapters or if it's still "you" who desires to manifest the wishes. If you still read this, and it made you angry or you found it vague and non-practical, I again encourage you to go back to the previous chapters and keep practicing the life without being caught up in the ego before revisiting this section again.

Chapter 7

3 Levels of Estate Planning

The Relative Still Matters

THIS CHAPTER IS about grounding the Teaching and the ultimate spiritual realization into our day-to-day reality, which for me is one of being an estate-planning attorney. One of the most common questions I'm asked by people who have not fully grasped the Teaching yet is this: If there is no separate self, if everything is one seamless reality, why does any of this human planning matter at all? Why plan for the future? Why prepare for death? Why write wills and trusts, if, in the deepest sense, nothing is ever born and nothing ever dies?

It's a fair question for those still caught up in the dichotomy of the reality, so I will attempt to answer it here. But as I said before, just because you've attained absolute realization, this human life does not just disappear; it goes on, but "your" reactions to it are now cohesive, precise, and undisturbed.

The Teaching described here is uncompromising at the absolute level: there is no individual doer, no separate entity, and no personal controller of life. And yet, the Teaching or non-dual traditions like Advaita in general are equally clear that as long as the body-mind is functioning in the world, the relative world does not disappear. Just because I've attained spiritual realization doesn't mean that this being/my avatar suddenly ends or goes on to exist in a vegetative state, to which any worldly activity is meaningless.

I am still a business owner and a mother in this reality, which still objectively exists. Bills still arrive. Children still depend on adults. Property still changes hands. Courts still operate. Suffering still occurs when preparation is absent. Yes, this suffering is seen as just a divine game of lila, but it still happens. Not being tied to it and knowing one's true nature does not mean we ignore death in the human world.

Non-dual knowledge does not erase the relative; it illuminates it. As I stated before, the path of full realization does not deny the worldly life—I cannot abandon my kids or stop being an attorney and let my whole life collapse into chaos; that would be spiritual nihilism, which still would be the ego trying to deny the worldly life. Think about it: if one finds full realization and now decides to abandon the life of a simple human, that is still the ego, as it still denies and separates by calling itself the "awakened" one and rejecting other aspects of the absolute reality as "wrong" or "non-awakened" or labeling the worldly life unholy.

No, the key here is to incorporate the knowledge into one's life, to illuminate the multitude of manifestations of God into effortless and beautiful being, regardless of what you do in your life.

In my worldly life, I plan people's estates. Coincidentally with my constant search for answers about life and death, I picked an area of law where I would be able to explore human relationships through the concept of dying or ending in some way. As a mother myself, I know firsthand how important it is to protect those you love the most, in case they lose a parent, a provider, or a teacher. Estate planning is so much more than just the legal documents. It is really about showing our true love and care for the ones who will be left behind, if this character in the movie of life should cease to exist.

Over years of working as an estate-planning attorney and years of walking the inner spiritual path, I began to see a parallel—the three levels of spiritual knowledge are very similar to the three levels of estate planning, starting from lower to higher. The way human beings approach estate planning mirrors the way the mind itself operates at different levels of maturity. (Remember the introductory chapter on the three levels of intellectual capacity and how those can perceive spiritual reality.)

> "A disorderly life makes a disorderly death."
>
> ~Seneca, *Letters to Lucilius*

The First, Most Basic Level: No Plan at All

At the most basic level is what we might call the reactive or unexamined mind, a beginner mind. This is the mind that clings to religious metaphors and avoids responsibility.

It is for such a type of mind that all the religious tales of gods, with detailed descriptions of their deeds and commandments, methods of worship, rituals, practices, and so forth were created. In fact, another world is created—in imagination. This mind lives entirely in the moment, driven by impulse, fear, avoidance, and habit. It does not like to think about death, incapacity, or responsibility.

Planning feels uncomfortable, so it is postponed indefinitely. "I'll deal with it later" becomes the unspoken mantra.

In estate-planning terms, this is the equivalent of no plan at all.

Somehow, even though everyone knows we are all mortal, a lot of people still avoid planning their estate. It's unfathomable to me, but irrational denial is a big problem in estate planning, as many people fear that even thinking about planning their estate will somehow make death come sooner.

Such denial and avoidance lead to a very unfortunate result: when such a person dies or becomes incapacitated, the consequences fall not on them, but on everyone else. Loved ones are left navigating courts, conflicts, delays, and costs. The absence of planning doesn't eliminate complexity; it transfers it to the people least equipped to handle it during moments of grief and shock.

Legally speaking, dying without an estate plan does not mean that everything somehow works itself out on its own. It means the State quietly steps in as the default planner. When no plan exists, the law imposes one through intestacy statutes, rigid formulas designed for administrative efficiency rather than human nuance.

These statutes do not know your family dynamics, your values, or your intentions. They do not account for the complexities of real relationships. They recognize only predefined legal categories such as spouse, child, or parent, often excluding stepchildren, unmarried partners, blended families, disabled beneficiaries, minors, or anyone who does not fit neatly into the statutory framework. The responsibility of handling the estate or becoming guardian for minor children is often placed on those who look the best on paper—criminal background and financial status, not the ones you would have chosen, if you could choose.

In the absence of a plan, assets are funneled through probate, a public court process that can be slow, costly, and emotionally draining. During this time, accounts may be frozen for months or even years, leaving loved ones without access to resources they may urgently need. Family members must petition the court for authority simply to act, while disputes, whether large or small, are resolved by judges rather than by the people who knew you best. Matters that were once private become part of the public record, accessible to anyone who cares to look.

And who even knows where to look for accounts or assets? Once probate authority is granted, it's on the personal representative to locate those, and that is not an easy job these days. Many assets pass through beneficiary designations, which may not have been updated, and may end up with an ex-spouse or a minor or a person who received Medicaid inheriting with no restrictions or possibilities to change or manage the assets.

I know a guy who inherited $2,000,000 from his ex-wife, as she failed to update her life insurance beneficiaries after divorce. The kids got nothing, as the life insurance was the only asset. Again, not planning leads to major mistakes like this, leaving our family completely blindsided—not only do they have to deal with the emotional aspect of grieving, but they now also need to deal with a public court process and financial aspects of not being able to carry on.

If incapacity occurs before death and no powers of attorney are in place, the consequences can be even more invasive. The court may appoint a guardian or conservator—someone you did not choose—to make decisions about your finances, your healthcare, and, in some cases, your body itself. From a human perspective, this represents the lowest level of responsibility, not because it is unethical or negligent in intent, but because it is unconscious of consequence.

The absence of planning does not remove complexity from life; it simply transfers that complexity to others at the moment when they are least prepared to carry it. If you became incapacitated today, who would you want to manage your legal, financial, and healthcare decisions for you? Your spouse? Your adult children? Your parents? Your best friend? In the absence of clear direction from you, they will all have to fight it out in court before the judge appoints the one who seems to be best suited (but may not be the person you would have chosen on your own).

And whoever ends up getting the job will now face the responsibility of trying to guess what you would have wanted! In the absence of clear instructions from you, that person will always live with a burden of having made a decision that could have affected the outcome of your treatment, your financial situation, or your life! Would you ever want your kids to have the burden of deciding whether to remove you from life support? Wouldn't they always live with a sense of guilt or second-guessing their decision? Would you want them to decide on amputations? Surgeries? Experimental treatments? The burden is unimaginable, and the absence of any directive only shows the selfishness of the one who didn't plan, as the consequences will be borne by the ones who are left to pick up the pieces.

See, estate planning is not about you at all. It's about those you love the most, and you owe it to them to make sure it's as easy as it can be on them, when they are dealing with the hardest loss of their lives. To avoid planning is not only irresponsible but very selfish.

I once worked with a woman whose life unraveled in a matter of weeks, not because of a lack of love, but because of a lack of preparation. Her husband was the primary breadwinner. He was healthy, hardworking, and in the middle of life. His death was sudden and completely unexpected (as if death can ever be expected, right?) But somehow, I hear this excuse a lot: "I am still young. I don't plan on dying."

The reality is we don't know when we are going to die, and death among the younger population is just as frequent as in the older one. With this client, her husband had no estate plan. No will. No trust. No life insurance. The house deed was in his name alone. All of the major bank accounts and investment accounts were titled solely to him.

When he died, everything stopped. Overnight, the wife found herself locked out of the very resources that had supported their family. Accounts were frozen as soon as the death certificate was issued. She could not access funds to pay the mortgage, utilities, or daily expenses. The house where she lived with their three minor children became legally untouchable. Even though she was his spouse, she had no authority to act without court approval. Being that she was a stay-at-home mom, she had no independent means of taking care of the bills, and they piled up quickly.

With no life insurance and no immediate access to assets, she fell behind on mortgage payments. The lender did not care that probate was pending or that funds were temporarily inaccessible. From their perspective, payments were simply not being made. Within months, foreclosure proceedings began.

The worst thing is that she (like many others) had no idea she needed to file for probate. She was too overwhelmed and crushed by grief to even think about going to consult with an attorney. Eventually, after the foreclosure, she realized she needed to start probate. With the help of an attorney, she had to petition the probate court to be appointed as personal representative of her own husband's estate.

That process took time—time she did not have. Filing fees, attorney costs, court delays, and required notices piled up, all while income had vanished and bills continued to arrive. By the time probate authority was finally granted, the damage had already been done. Legal costs had drained what little liquidity remained, and the house, once the center of her children's sense of safety, was lost. What could have been a period of grief and adjustment became a crisis of survival, all because there was no plan in place to bridge the gap between death and continuity.

What haunts me most about stories like this is not just what happened, but what *could* have happened, as both parents failed to plan in this case! If both parents had died in that accident, the situation would have been even more devastating. With no named guardians, the decision of who would care for their children would not have belonged to family—it would have belonged to the court. A judge, working from limited information and under time pressure, would have been tasked with deciding where the children should live. Competing relatives could have stepped forward, triggering investigations, hearings, and conflict. If no suitable guardian was immediately available, or if disputes arose, the children could have been placed temporarily in foster care while the court sorted it out.

This process is not gentle. It involves background checks, home studies, interviews, and legal proceedings that can stretch on for months. Children who have already lost their parents may be moved between homes, separated from siblings, or placed with strangers, not because anyone wants that outcome, but because the system requires procedure before certainty. None of this happens because the parents failed to love their children. It happens because they assumed there would always be more time.

This is why planning matters - not as a fear-based exercise, but as an act of protection. An estate plan does not prevent tragedy, but it can prevent tragedy from multiplying. It creates continuity where there would otherwise be collapse. It ensures that, in moments of loss, families are held by structure rather than overwhelmed by chaos. No one plans because they expect to die. They plan because they care about what happens when they do.

"No plan survives contact with reality."
~Attributed to Helmuth von Moltke the Elder

Middle Level: The Will-Based Plan

At the next level is the intermediate mind. This mind's attention is captured by the idea of transformation. There are still concepts of transforming, reincarnation, and karma. That means judgment and relative qualities still remain; subject and object remain.

This mind recognizes responsibility but tends to operate at the level of convention. It does what it has seen others do. It asks, "What is expected of me?" rather than, "What is actually needed?"

This is the mind that writes a simple will, names beneficiaries, and assumes that should be sufficient.

In estate-planning terms, this corresponds to a will-based plan.

A will is not wrong. It is an improvement. It reflects awareness that life ends and preparation matters. But it still operates reactively and overlooks many of the important what-ifs or practical considerations. It relies on courts. It leaves room for disputes. It assumes everything will unfold cleanly, even though experience tells us otherwise.

A will is often described as "having a plan," and in one important sense, that is true. A will reflects awareness. It acknowledges that life ends and that responsibility extends beyond it. Compared to having no plan at all, a will is a meaningful step forward. But over years of practice, I have learned that a will alone rarely does what people believe it will do.

It is the simplest plan you can create, one where you don't spend much time contemplating what would actually happen on a practical level, but rather you do it just to check the box—a bare minimum effort. For a person who picks a will, it's like choosing the path of least resistance—when presented with options of no planning, will planning, or trust planning, they pick the middle grounds, as it is "good enough," cheap, and still gets the "estate planning" box checked on their bucket list. But they miss the multitude of potential implications.

Typically, a will states, "I leave everything to so-and-so." But who knows what that "everything" is? Deeds, bank accounts, life insurance? A will does not gather assets. It does not locate accounts. It does not unlock access. It is a set of generic instructions written on paper, waiting for someone else—often in the midst of grief—to bring it to life. And that someone is usually a personal representative who has never done this before, who is emotionally overwhelmed, and who suddenly bears the legal responsibility of reconstructing another person's entire financial life.

Most people do not leave behind a neat list of what they own. Accounts are scattered across institutions. Some are forgotten. Some were opened decades earlier. Some are digital, some physical, some joint, and some individual. Retirement accounts, bank accounts, brokerage accounts, employer benefits, old life insurance policies, safety deposit boxes, online assets—none of these are automatically connected to a will.

Often, when I meet with clients, even spouses who have been married for many years do not have a full picture of what the other spouse owns! And if your spouse doesn't know, how would anyone else find the "everything" you mentioned in your will? The executor must find them, identify them, value them, and then determine how each one is supposed to pass.

And all of this happens through probate. Until the court formally appoints the executor, they have no authority to act. They cannot access accounts, pay bills, sell property, or even obtain full information from financial institutions. Time passes. Expenses continue. Stress compounds. What was meant to be a straightforward act of care becomes a scavenger hunt under pressure. And who wants to go through a court process when they are grieving?

Even when a will is clear, it is still subject to interpretation, challenge, and delay. Probate is a public process. Filings are required. Notices must be sent. Deadlines must be met. Family members, already raw with grief, may disagree about meaning, fairness, or intent. The executor is placed in the impossible position of being both a mourner and a manager, both family member and fiduciary.

And another big thing—a will does not control all of your assets. Joint ownership and beneficiary designations actually override the will. Remember the guy who got $2,000,000 from his ex-wife's life insurance? There was no probate in that case, which means, even if she had a will that said, "I leave everything to my kids," but that "everything" was just the life insurance that had her ex-husband as a beneficiary, her kids would get nothing after probating the will.

That's why it's so important to review all of your assets as part of your estate-planning conversation. Simply stating, "I leave everything to..." is just not enough.

And perhaps most importantly, a will does nothing during incapacity. If someone becomes ill, injured, or cognitively impaired but remains alive, the will offers no help. The same court involvement is required, the same delays occur, and the same stress is imposed—this time while the person is still living.

I once worked with a family who believed they had done everything "right." Their father had a will. It was properly signed, witnessed, and stored. He had even talked about it openly, assuring his children that everything was taken care of and there would be no problems when the time came. When he died, they quickly learned how fragile that belief was.

The will left his estate to his children in equal shares. On paper, it seemed simple. But almost immediately, questions arose that the will did not—and could not—answer. Some assets passed through probate. Others did not. Several accounts had beneficiary designations that had never been updated after his divorce years earlier. A retirement account still named a former spouse. A life insurance policy named a sibling to whom he had stopped speaking decades ago. Those assets passed automatically, outside the will, to people he would never have chosen at the end of his life.

The children were stunned. They assumed the will controlled everything. It didn't. At the same time, the probate process began to stretch on. Before anything could be accessed or distributed, the court had to appoint a personal representative. Notices had to be sent. Deadlines had to be met. Financial institutions demanded certified documents, court orders, and weeks of processing time. Meanwhile, bills kept coming. Property taxes were due. Maintenance costs piled up. Emotions ran high.

Probate also did something more subtle but far more damaging: it turned private grief into a public process. Every filing was visible. Every disagreement had a legal stage. Family members who might have quietly accepted outcomes in a private trust setting now had an incentive to object, question, and contest—because the system allowed it and sometimes encouraged it.

Old resentments surfaced. One child questioned whether certain gifts had really been intended to be "equal." Another argued that they had provided more care and should be compensated. A distant relative appeared, asserting rights they had never mentioned while the father was alive. What began as mourning slowly morphed into negotiation, then accusation.

It's funny how clients always assure me that their kids get along great and "would never fight" over money. But in 99% of the cases, they do, as it's just human nature. People change when they grieve, and they also change when money is involved. Egos run wild, sadly.

Months turned into over a year. Legal fees mounted—not because anyone was greedy, but because every step required professional help, and every sibling felt like they needed representation, because otherwise they would be shorted. Each had a spouse. That's a major thing most clients don't realize—even if you think your kids would never fight, are you also confident that their *spouses* won't? In this case, spouses egged the parties on, insisting they each take what "they are owed" and stirring conflict in sibling relationships already strained by grief and court.

Appraisals had to be ordered. Hearings scheduled. Motions filed. Each delay meant more stress, more expense, and more emotional depletion. The children found themselves spending weekends sorting through paperwork instead of memories, arguing over receipts instead of healing.

By the time the estate was finally closed, much of what their father had worked to leave behind had been reduced by court costs, attorney fees, and unnecessary losses. But the deeper cost was relational. The siblings no longer trusted one another. Conversations became formal, guarded, and infrequent. What could have been a shared period of remembrance became a prolonged experience of tension and fatigue. The spouses who got involved were resented by other siblings, and the family quickly turned into strangers who only interacted out of necessity.

Their father had not failed to plan. He had simply stopped too soon; taken a shortcut instead of going the long way. Again, it's easy to take a shortcut when you see no practical implications of your lack of planning during life—it only unravels after you are gone.

A will expressed his intention, but it did not account for the full complexity of his life. It did not coordinate beneficiary designations. It did not prevent conflict. It did not protect the family from delay, exposure, or emotional strain. It left too many decisions to a system designed to resolve disputes, not preserve relationships. And it was also not kept up to date, which is another major thing we stress with our clients—your life changes: divorces, kids, grandkids, new assets, and your plan needs to reflect those changes, too. Otherwise, it will almost certainly fail when it is needed most.

This is the quiet truth about will-based planning. It is better than no plan. But it often assumes a simplicity that real life rarely offers. And when that assumption collapses, it is the family—not the paperwork—that absorbs the impact.

This is why I often say that a will is better than no plan, but it is still a plan that assumes everything will go smoothly and that someone else will have the capacity, clarity, and resilience to carry it out. In reality, the burden of execution falls on people at the very moment when their ability to shoulder it is most compromised.

A will expresses intention, but it does not create continuity. It names outcomes, but it does not build the structure needed to reach them. And when structure is absent, even the best intentions can unravel.

This is not a failure of morality or effort; it's just a mediocre effort at best. And it is simply a mismatch between what a will can do and what modern life actually requires.

"Just as a skilled physician treats illness before it arises, the wise remove suffering before it appears."

~Buddhist teaching
(paraphrased from the Pali Canon)

Mature, Highest Level: A Trust-Based Plan

Then, there is the mature or advanced mind. This mind is pure and does not associate itself with concepts, while not rejecting them. Nothing needs to be rejected or transformed.

This mind has the potential to truly grasp the spiritual teaching in this book. The self is one and the same as God, the Universe, and all creation. This mind does not plan out of fear but out of clarity. It sees beyond itself. It understands systems, consequences, and interdependence. It recognizes that love expressed in advance is one of the most powerful forms of care. This mind plans not because it is attached to control, but because it understands responsibility within the relative world.

In estate-planning terms, this is a trust-based plan.

A trust is not about clinging to assets or extending identity beyond death. It is about reducing friction. It is about continuity. It is about minimizing unnecessary suffering. It is about making sure that when the body is gone or the mind is compromised, life can keep flowing

www.ingramcontent.com/pod-product-compliance
Lightning Source LLC
LaVergne TN
LVHW090406210926
848480LV00002B/468

smoothly for those who remain. It is about the people you love the most.

A revocable living trust is a legal structure that allows you to place your assets under the management of a trust during your lifetime, while still retaining full control over them by letting you remain the trustee of your own trust. You can amend it, revoke it, or change its terms at any time while you are alive and competent. Unlike a will, which only becomes effective after death and must be carried out through probate, a revocable living trust operates continuously.

Assets that are properly titled in the trust are managed by a trustee you choose after your death, without court involvement. This continuity is what makes a trust fundamentally different—and more effective—than a will. Because the trust does not die, there is no need for probate, no public court process, no freezing of accounts, and no delay before action can be taken. Bills can be paid, property can be managed or sold, and distributions can occur immediately and privately. In this way, a revocable living trust does not merely express intention, as a will does; it creates a functioning framework that carries those intentions forward seamlessly, reducing conflict, expense, and stress for the people you leave behind.

You are the one who pre-does all of the work: you look at your assets, how they are titled, how they are beneficiary designated, and you make sure that your trust is properly reflected in each and every one of your assets. Your trust also provides for contingencies, unlike simple beneficiary designations, meaning that even if your first beneficiary dies, the trust will still keep the asset out of probate and give it to the one next in line.

A trust also helps avoid conflict, as there is no public court process your family has to deal with, and it is extremely hard to challenge a trust, so your family is left to carry out your final specific and detailed wishes. A trust lets you leave a conscious legacy, one that will echo through multiple generations, as it carries forward the level of love and care you took, and your loved ones are left with a simple set of to-dos, while not being subject to the court's timeline or having to look for what you meant when you said "everything."

What makes a trust truly effective, however, is not just its creation but its ongoing maintenance. A trust only governs the assets that are actually titled into it, which means that, as life changes—e.g., new accounts are opened, properties are purchased, businesses are formed, marriages begin or end—the plan must be updated to reflect those changes. Without ongoing guidance, even a well-drafted trust can slowly lose alignment with reality, leaving gaps that undermine its purpose.

This is why working with a firm that treats estate planning as a long-term relationship rather than a one-time transaction is essential. Proper planning includes regular reviews, funding guidance, and proactive updates, so the trust continues to function as intended. When maintained correctly, a revocable living trust becomes a living framework that adapts alongside your life, preserving continuity, avoiding probate, and ensuring that your intentions remain clear and effective, no matter how circumstances change.

I worked with a lady for whom I helped set up a revocable living trust in 2021. A mother with adult children. A blended family. Multiple accounts spread across institutions. Real estate, retirement funds, and personal property with both financial and sentimental value. The difference was not in the complexity of her life, but in how it was structured ahead of time.

When she came to our firm, we created a trust for her and, just as importantly, funded it. Accounts were retitled into the trust. Beneficiary designations were reviewed and coordinated. The trust laid out a clear roadmap—not only for who would receive assets, but for how decisions would be made, by whom, and in what order. Tangible personal property was addressed specifically, including items that could easily have become sources of conflict if left undefined.

Unfortunately, she passed away just recently, in 2025. When she died, there was no scramble. The trustee stepped in immediately, without court involvement, petitions, or delay. Bills were paid on time. Property was managed seamlessly. No accounts were frozen. There were no public filings, no waiting periods, and no probate calendar dictating the family's next move.

Life continued with a quiet stability that allowed the family to grieve rather than manage. The trustee (her adult child) requested a call with me to make sure she was administering the trust correctly. When we spoke, she outlined what she had done and how she planned to proceed, and when I confirmed she had been doing everything correctly, she gave out a huge sigh and exclaimed, "Is it really that easy? I requested a call with you because I was sure I was missing something, that I needed to go file something with a court or wait out some sort of a delay."

This statement warmed my heart, as it truly shows the value of what I do and why it matters so much. Because the plan had been thoughtfully designed in advance, there was little room for interpretation. Distributions were clear. Authority was clear. Expectations were clear. There was no incentive to contest the plan, because there was no public probate process to contest it in. Conversations happened privately, within the family, rather than through attorneys, pleadings, and court hearings.

Granted, the trustee was sad and a bit distraught, having just lost her mother, but her mom's plan eased what could have been a much heavier burden to carry after losing a loved one. And that is what true estate planning is all about—making it as easy as possible for those you love the most, when you are no longer there to guide them.

Perhaps most importantly, no single family member was burdened with an impossible role. The trustee acted as a stabilizing presence, following clear instructions rather than improvising under pressure. No one had to reconstruct their mother's financial life or guess at her wishes. She had already done that work herself.

The contrast to the prior story about probate was striking. Where probate turns grief into administration, the trust allowed grief to remain what it is: human, personal, and temporary. Where a will invites interpretation, the trust provided continuity. Where a public process often amplifies old tensions, the trust quietly dissolved them by removing the stage altogether.

Nothing about this plan prevented loss. But it prevented loss from multiplying into chaos. She did not create the trust to control the future. She created it to remove unnecessary friction from it. And in doing so, she left behind not only assets, but a final, living expression of care—one that continued to function long after she was gone.

Why This Matters Even in Non-Dual Understanding

Here is the subtle point that often gets missed: non-dual realization does not absolve the human system of its relative impact.

Yes, at the absolute level, there is no individual who owns anything. But at the relative level, property exists, children exist, spouses exist, and legal systems exist. Ignoring this does not make one enlightened. It makes one unavailable, and it creates an entitled ego who is too good for the human form.

In Advaita, this is sometimes expressed as the distinction between paramārthika satya (ultimate truth) and vyavahārika satya (transactional truth). Confusing the two can lead to spiritual bypassing. Integrating them leads to wisdom.

These are not competing realities, and one does not cancel out the other. They describe the same life seen from different depths. Remember, Advaita literally means "not two," so while these two aspects of reality cannot be separated, both must be equally honored as God's (our) cherished creation.

Paramārthika satya is the ultimate truth: from this level, there is only one reality—pure consciousness, Brahman, awareness itself. There is no separate self, no true division, no birth or death in an absolute sense. Everything that appears—bodies, thoughts, feelings, events, time, and even the sense of "I"—is seen as a temporary appearance within a single, seamless field. From this perspective, nothing is ever truly lost, harmed, or incomplete. Nothing and no one dies, as nothing exists as a separate self-lasting entity. This is the truth pointed to by non-dual realization discussed in great detail in this book.

Vyavahārika satya is the transactional truth: the level at which human life actually functions. At this level, people have names, families, bodies, responsibilities, and legal systems. Hunger still needs food. Children still need care. Money still pays bills. Courts still exist. Cause and effect still operate. Time still goes on; bodies get born, live, and die. Even after awakening, the body continues to live in this realm.

Ignoring this level does not make it disappear; it simply creates unnecessary suffering—it is a way for the ego to confirm itself once again, by rejecting the worldly life as non-real. But in reality, it still arises in Brahman and is just as real as the body that it lives through. There is no denying that for a rational thinker.

A simple way to understand the relationship is this: ultimate truth explains what is real; transactional truth explains how life works. Knowing that a movie is "just a movie" does not mean you stop following the plot while you are watching it. In the same way, realizing that the self is not ultimately real does not remove the practical consequences of actions taken, or not taken, within the human world.

Once you find yourself as the screen on which the movie is playing out, the character you mistakenly thought yourself to be continues its storyline in the movie, you just stop identifying yourself with that character and find yourself as the screen, which will not move or be affected, even if the movie ends and the character dies.

Advaita and our Teaching does not ask us to choose one truth over the other. Wisdom lies in holding both at once. From the ultimate perspective, there is nothing to control and nothing to protect. From the transactional perspective, care, foresight, and responsibility still matter deeply.

This world is woven out of God, and denying or rejecting its flow is analogous to rejecting God. Confusing the two leads to bypassing, which is a trick of the ego—using spiritual insight to avoid practical responsibility. In simple words: ultimate truth tells you who you really are; transactional truth tells you how to live wisely as a human being. Integrating them leads to maturity—living with clarity at the deepest level while acting skillfully at the human one without possessing or controlling it.

That is the true key to the end of suffering in the human form. Nothing needs to be fixed at the level of truth, but at the level of life, things still need attention.

Estate planning is not about death. It is about care. It is about recognizing that, while the "I" may dissolve, relationships and responsibilities continue in form. Planning is an act of compassion, not control.

Why I Do This Work

I do this work because I have seen what happens when people don't plan; and I've seen that it has nothing to do with intelligence, spirituality, or goodness. I have worked with families who loved each other deeply and were torn apart simply because no structure was put in place ahead of time. I have watched courts replace conversations and conflict replace clarity. Having gone through immigration and seeing how fragile our worldly possessions are, I never want my kids to be at the mercy of a public court judge or to have to struggle while the legal system freezes that which I meant to leave for them.

Knowing that there is no separate self does not make me less committed to helping people plan. It makes me more committed. Because I see clearly that suffering is unnecessary; and unnecessary suffering is worth preventing.

A well-crafted estate plan is not a contradiction of non-duality. It is its expression in form.

Just as awareness moves through the body with working intelligence, planning moves through the legal world with foresight. One does not negate the other. They operate at different levels of the same reality.

Estate planning is not about securing the future. It is about removing obstacles from it. And that, even in a seamless, indivisible reality, still matters.

If the only realization you take away from this book is the fact that you owe it to your loved ones to get your estate planning done, I am still elated and hope you take the next step in developing your personal plan.

Chapter 8

Why this Book is the Ultimate, Non-compromising, Radical Truth

HAVING ARRIVED AT the final chapter, I congratulate you, dear reader, as you will never be as you were before you picked up this book. Regardless of the level of depth this knowledge has seeped into you yet, your true nature has recognized this as the ultimate truth and will continue building on this realization, until the Teaching is fully internalized and becomes your life every waking and sleeping second and beyond.

Granted, some of you may be overwhelmed with information and have more questions. As I already stated, your ego will likely revolt, and you will be forced to step away from this knowledge temporarily and busy yourself with the ego games. But eventually, this knowledge you now have glimpsed will call you back to practicing it and to realizing its truth in your own practical experience.

Among the many questions your ego will likely flood you with (but if you are still earnest, honest, and attentive, these logistical questions will fall away, as this book literally leaves no stone unturned; and if you were earnest, honest, and attentive when reading it, there would be no more questions left) will still be the one that is meant to doubt the foundation of you getting this information, i.e. the source, or me.

"Why listen to her?" your ego asks. "Is she an awakened guru of some sort? Does she have the credibility and the years of meditating in an ashram hidden in the Himalayas? Does she possess any certification of a spiritual guru or a life coach?" She is just an attorney, after all, very down-to-earth, practical, and far from attaining any accolades in the spiritual community.

All of those are fair questions to ask. The answer is that this knowledge does not belong to me, Pasha, Maharaj, Buddha, Jesus, or any other name, as this knowledge itself gets rid of the concept of authorship or possession.

However, if you, like me, have ever explored other non-dualistic spiritual traditions, such as Advaita Vedānta, Dzogchen Buddhism, any aspects of yoga, or even Christian Scripture, you will find the concepts outlined in this book echoing through all of them. Many of the ancient texts are kept sacred and secret; many are not even allowed to be translated into English or any other languages; and many that were translated are very hard to navigate or discern. The knowledge outlined here simplifies these intricate non-dualistic ideas, finds support for them in modern science, and presents them in an organized, easy to understand way, making high spiritual realization available to all seekers.

If you still need verification, I will quote various traditions below, to demonstrate that all non-dualistic spiritual gurus, across times, locations, ethnicities, languages, and cultures, spoke of the same truth—the one that you are lucky enough to have discovered in this lifetime. See, when our collective non-dual consciousness

(God/Universe) first manifested itself through the Big Bang into billions of shapes, particles, creatures, etc., it took time for the pieces of the one to find their way back to the original source. Some parts never made it, some found the realization but were unable to express it in human language, and those who did both are now the eternally recognized gurus of the highest of spiritual traditions. In different parts of its own vast creation, the one voice of God echoes across ages, cultures, and languages:

Ramana Maharshi, a South Indian sage who taught through silence as much as words, said, "The self is not something to be reached. You are already the Self." For Ramana, liberation was not an achievement but a recognition that awareness is not located in the body or mind. It is the space in which both arise.

Centuries earlier, Adi Shankaracharya, the great systematizer of Advaita, expressed the same insight: "Brahman[4] is real. The world is an appearance. The individual self is not different from Brahman." In his teachings, what appears as a personal life, with choices and struggles, is ultimately a misidentification within a single, indivisible reality.

The Ashtavakra Gita, one of the most uncompromising Advaita texts, says, "You are not the doer nor the enjoyer. You are pure awareness." Here, samsara is not escaped by

---

[4] Brahman is the absolute reality; the infinite, formless ground of all existence. In Advaita Vedānta, Brahman is not a god among other gods, not a being with preferences or personality, and not an object that can be perceived. Brahman is that which makes perception possible. It is pure being, pure knowing, pure presence, limitless, timeless, and indivisible.

better choices, but is dissolved by seeing that the chooser was never real.

This same truth appears in the ancient Upanishads, where the Brihadaranyaka Upanishad asks, "Where there is duality, one sees another. But where everything has become the Self, what is there to see?" The question is rhetorical: when separation collapses, there is no one left to stand apart from experience.

In Dzogchen Buddhism, the language changes, but the realization remains identical. Padmasambhava, the teacher who brought Dzogchen to Tibet, described the human mind as "empty in essence, luminous in nature, and unimpeded in manifestation." Emptiness here does not mean nothingness; it means openness—the same living space this book points to again and again.

His philosophical heir, Longchenpa, wrote poetically that there is "nothing to abandon, nothing to cultivate, nothing to realize beyond what already is." Realization is resting as the field, not fixing its contents.

Modern Advaita voices echo this with simplicity meant for modern-day seekers. Nisargadatta Maharaj, a former cigarette vendor turned teacher, said, "You are not a person. You are the awareness in which the person appears." The sense of ego, choice, and agency is seen not as an enemy, but as an appearance, like a wave in one vast ocean of who we are, never separate from the ocean itself.

Similarly, Papaji reduced the entire path to a single instruction: "Stop. There is nothing to do. Be quiet." This one line, directing one to be quiet, is the epitome of wisdom and is something that my Teacher Pasha, would always urge us to do: let go of thoughts and simply be still and quiet, internally.

Closer to our modern times, world-renowned Western thinkers arrived at the same insight, often without religious language. Jiddu Krishnamurti, educated in the West but fiercely anti-authority, stated bluntly, "Choice itself is confusion," and, "When the observer is the observed, conflict ends." For Krishnamurti, the division between self and world was the root of suffering, and its dissolution was freedom.

In Christianity, the most widespread Western religion, the concepts of non-duality and the illusion of ego permeate the religious teachings in subtle ways, yet very obvious to advanced minds. Meister Eckhart (13th-14th c.) is the clearest and boldest about this: "The more completely you give yourself to God, the more he gives himself to you." And even more directly, "Let God be God in you."

Another foundational Christian framing comes from Saint Augustine. Strikingly concisely, he confirms everything the non-dual traditions teach: "God is closer to us than we are to ourselves."

And from Scripture itself, which underlies the whole idea: "Not I, but Christ lives in me." (Galatians 2:20)

Jesus Christ Himself spoke so precisely on this, echoing the non-dual traditions:

> *I am the light that is over all things.*
> *I am all: from me all came forth, and to me all attained.*
> *Split a piece of wood; I am there.*
> *Lift up the stone, and you will find me there.*
>
> —Gospel of Thomas, Saying 77

Isn't this the exact summary of what this whole book is about? God equals the all-pervading space that everything consists of—rocks, wood, our bodies. From that space/God, all came forth, and to it all attained.

Seen together, these voices converge on a single recognition: there is no independent ego choosing life from the outside. Beginner minds simply misinterpret all of these teachings by assigning the separate ego as the "interpreter" of these highest truths. All of these teaching sound in Unison: What we truly are is the empty, luminous space—call it Brahman, awareness, nature, the Universe, quantum field, or God—in which all choices, thoughts, worlds, and bodies arise. Ultimate realization is not becoming something greater; it is discovering that the space you have been standing in all along is what the sages were pointing to, and which is what we are.

Modern-day scientific advancements echo the ancient non-dual teachings. Albert Einstein himself echoed the same intuition when he wrote that the sense of being a separate self is "a kind of optical delusion of consciousness," and that freedom lies in expanding one's identity beyond the personal.

In physics, the closer we look at matter, the less solid and independent it becomes. At the deepest levels, particles are no longer "things" but probabilities—vibrations in fields that cannot be separated from the space in which they arise. Space itself turns out not to be empty but seething with potential, indistinguishable from energy and form.

In neuroscience, experiments now consistently show that decisions arise in the brain before we become conscious of "making" them, undermining the idea of a personal chooser directing life from the center. Conscious awareness registers actions, thoughts, and intentions, but does not initiate them. Even biology reflects this unity: the atoms in our bodies were forged in ancient stars, the same processes that shaped distant galaxies, leaving no meaningful boundary between "us" and the universe we perceive.

Across disciplines, the conclusion converges with the sages' insight: what we call mind, matter, choice, and self are not separate agents acting on reality, but movements within a single, indivisible field. Science does not yet speak the language of Brahman or God, but it is quietly confirming the same truth: that there is one seamless reality, appearing as many, known from within as awareness itself.

So, if your ego does not trust me, a humble attorney turned spiritual seeker, look into the vast body of teachings that were created years, lifetimes, centuries, and millennia ago, along with the developments in twenty-first-century science, to truly confirm, once and for all, that the individual "you" never existed; that the concept of choice is an illusion, and that the only way to achieve full realization and immortality is to realize God is one seamless, borderless reality, in which we all arise, last, and disappear, but our true self/God never moves.

You do have the option, of course, to still not trust me or the Teaching, and to carry on with playing the divine lila[5] until your mind is ready to internalize the knowledge and is tired of playing the cyclical games of samsara. You can still live from the ego, assign blame, suffer, pay a therapist

[5] Līlā in Sanskrit means "divine play" or "cosmic game." In Advaita and broader Hindu philosophy, it describes the way the Absolute (Brahman) appears as the universe not out of necessity, lack, or purpose, but out of freedom, creativity, and delight.

thousands of dollars to treat "your" trauma, work on embracing "your" shadow, attempt to forgive "your" ancestors, and attempt to embrace "your" flaws and failures. But all of these will bring you only temporary relief, and the moment your ego is triggered by another wrongdoer, all your work will collapse momentarily.

I am not writing this to negate or downplay therapy and all the other types of spiritual work—they all exist and have their place, just as everything else does in this world woven out of God. Every aspect of it is divine, as it is all made from the same God. All I mean is to invite those of you who are tired of playing the lila game of samsara and who want eternal peace and harmony to stay still, shine the light of your awareness into every truth uncovered by this book, confirm it in your practical experience, and finally arrive home.

And that requires you to accept the Teaching, not by way of a dogma, but through practical experience, honesty, and clear logical thinking, as the ultimate (you arrive where you started), radical (there are no other ways to explain the Universe), and non-compromising (if you are honest with yourself, there is no word game you can play to deny what you find) Truth.

Namaste.[6]

---

6 Namaste in Sanskrit means *"I bow to you."* Spiritually, namaste carries the recognition that what is being bowed to is not the person's role or identity, but the same awareness, the same Brahman, looking out through different forms.

Conclusion

"Unchanging from the beginning…
Without transfer or change…
To just recognize this fundamental nature of self
is summed up in the name 'buddha.'
By realizing this essence, with no phenomena to invite or prevent,
everything is pervasively even in the sole dharmata[7].
Like an island of gold, there is nothing to discern or exclude."

~Omniscient Longchenpa,
"Jewel Treasure of the Dharmadhatu"
translated by Lama Chonam and Sangye Khandro.

AFTER ALMOST TWO years of internalizing and living and breathing the Teaching that my precious Teacher Pasha has given me, which I've tried to relay to my fullest ability in this book, I was finally ready to turn to the Jewel Treasure of the Dharmadhatu, a quote from which I chose to end this book, as it sums up the full reality of our existence—never beginning, never ending, with no boundaries, no labels, no

[7] Dharmatā literally means "suchness," "naturalness," or "the way things truly are." In Buddhism, it represents the inherent nature of things, as they truly are.

concepts and no limitations. One true awareness is whatever truly is.

For an unprepared mind, reading this book will just seem like elevated, creative, and beautiful poetry, but once you are familiarized with the Teaching, you see it as a direct pointing to reality as it is, before division, before effort, before a path even begins.

At its core, the text describes dharmadhātu—the all-encompassing expanse in which all phenomena arise and dissolve, as already complete, already pure, already awake. Nothing needs to be corrected or transcended. Thoughts, emotions, bodies, worlds, and identities are not obstacles to truth; they are truth appearing in motion. Awareness does not stand apart from experience. It is the very substance of experience itself. In this way, what we normally call confusion is simply clarity misunderstood, and suffering is awareness forgetting its own nature while never actually leaving it.

The Jewel Treasure, just like this book (I hope), attempts to return you again and again to a single recognition: there is no separate practitioner and no separate goal. Effort aimed at attaining realization subtly assumes lack, while true realization begins with the recognition of fullness. Space is not empty; it is luminous. Emptiness is not absence; it is infinite potential. Forms do not obscure awareness; they are awareness expressing itself. Nothing is rejected. Nothing needs improving. Nothing is outside, as there is no outside.

Once you internalize the Teaching, I encourage you to read the Jewel Treasure, as it is a beautiful, poetic revelation of the highest non-dual teaching available to humans, and to keep it for reference each time the ego creeps in and attempts to disrupt the harmony.

What I hope the readers will take from this book is complete and final liberation; end of suffering, and end of looking and anticipating; the falling off of the "spiritual path" and full realization that the path and the path taker are one. Understand that liberation is not an event in time but a recognition outside time that the quiet certainty that what is looking for truth is itself the truth.

There is nothing to fix at the absolute level, yet life continues to unfold at the relative level as care, responsibility, and expression. The highest spiritual truth is not an escape from the world, but a deep permission for the world to be exactly as it is, known from the inside as liberation itself.

Namaskar.[8]

---

[8] In Sanskrit, an act of bowing, not as submission, but as humility before what is greater and shared. In simple terms, *Namaskar* says, "What I truly am recognizes what you truly are."

Afterword

DEAR READER,

I bow to you for having completed the journey without the journey-taker and having arrived at the point of your fullest realization! As my dear Teacher Pasha, would say, at the point when you finally find yourself and arrive home, someone (God) is quietly smiling, and you find yourself the essence of that peaceful, loving, caring, and kind smile. I truly hope this book helped you end suffering once and for all, escape the loop of constant pain and pleasure cycles, and finally rest in your own peaceful essence.

I understand, however, that for some of you, reading the book, even in full earnestness and with full dedication and attention, is not quite enough to fully get you to the state you need to be. Multiple variables (your environment, people around you, your levels of stress, etc.) may affect your journey, and for some, it can take longer than for others. This is why I offer to those who would benefit from some direct guidance, my in-person or online retreats.

This book itself has everything you need to attain full realization, but being in the presence of others on the same path may speed up the process and help you achieve full realization. Granted, just reading this book, even if you haven't fully internalized the Teaching yet, has caused major changes in the way you look at the world. You will never be able to forget the truth once you come across it, and you will see major substantive changes in every aspect of your life, guaranteed.

For those of you who do want to continue the journey or need some extra support, I welcome you to join my coaching/retreats, (I cannot quite figure out what to call this process, as it is truly neither a retreat nor coaching, but for the sake of having a name, let's just refer to it as such.) You can scan the QR code below.

Or go to www.anastasiafainberg.org.

And of course, for those of you who have not planned their estates yet, I invite you to take care of the most important thing you can do for your family. If you are in Colorado, simply go to www.legacylawgroupcolorado.com to get started.

I hope to meet some of you soon, but to all of you, I want to say that I love myself in you beyond measure. Namaskar.

About the Author

ANASTASIA FAINBERG writes at the intersection of law, science, consciousness, and lived experience. She is the founder and principal attorney of Legacy Law Group Colorado, PLLC, a boutique estate-planning and asset-protection law firm, where she guides families through some of life's most tangible thresholds: incapacity, inheritance, continuity, and the quiet questions of what we leave behind. Day after day, she witnesses how love can be expressed not only through feeling, but through structure; the practical decisions that prevent unnecessary suffering and protect the people we cherish.

Beneath her legal work runs a lifelong spiritual inquiry. Anastasia has studied multiple religious traditions, exploring the nature of identity, awareness, and the mysterious boundary where the timeless meets the everyday. Her writing reflects this integration: the precision of a legal mind paired with contemplative depth, bringing the reader back again and again to direct experience of space, presence, and the dissolving of the separate self.

An immigrant and attorney by training, Anastasia brings a comparative perspective to both her legal and spiritual work. Having lived between cultures and legal systems, she developed an early sensitivity to how identity, belonging, and security are shaped, not only by inner narratives but by external structures. Earning her law degree and building her practice in the United States, she learned firsthand how systems can either fracture families in moments of crisis or quietly safeguard them. That dual lens, personal and professional, insider and outsider, deeply informs her writing.

This book was born not from knowledge alone, but from love, first revealed to her through her children, Daniel, Raphael, and Adele. In their presence, she encountered a kind of unconditional love that asked nothing in return, and from that encounter, a larger question emerged: How can this same love be lived without condition, for everyone? These pages are her exploration of that question and an offering that holds both truths at once: the ultimate recognition that nothing is missing, and the human responsibility to live, love, and plan with care.

Anastasia's websites:
www.anastasiafainberg.org
www.legacylawgroupcolorado.com
Her social media accounts:
@beyond.the.I_
@legacylawgroup (Instagram).